REDWORK

from The WORKBASKET

REBECCA KEMP BRENT

KRAUSE PUBLICATIONS
CINCINNATI, OHIO

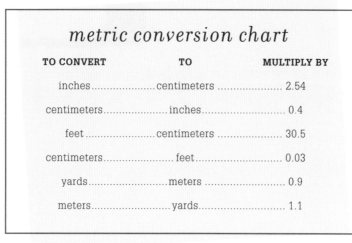

metric conversion chart

TO CONVERT	TO	MULTIPLY BY
inches	centimeters	2.54
centimeters	inches	0.4
feet	centimeters	30.5
centimeters	feet	0.03
yards	meters	0.9
meters	yards	1.1

14 13 12 11 10   5 4 3 2 1

DISTRIBUTED IN CANADA BY FRASER DIRECT
100 Armstrong Avenue
Georgetown, ON, Canada L7G 5S4
Tel: (905) 877-4411

DISTRIBUTED IN THE U.K. AND EUROPE BY DAVID & CHARLES
Brunel House, Newton Abbot, Devon, TQ12 4PU, England
Tel: (+44) 1626 323200, Fax: (+44) 1626 323319
E-mail: postmaster@davidandcharles.co.uk

DISTRIBUTED IN AUSTRALIA BY CAPRICORN LINK
P.O. Box 704, S. Windsor NSW, 2756 Australia
Tel: (02) 4577-3555

Library of Congress Cataloging in Publication Data
Brent, Rebecca Kemp.
  Redwork from The WORKBASKET / Rebecca Kemp Brent.
  -- 1st ed.
    p. cm.
  Includes bibliographical references and index.
  ISBN 978-0-89689-972-8 (pbk. : alk. paper)
  1. Embroidery, Machine--Patterns. 2. Redwork. 3. Quilting.
    I. Workbasket. II. Title.
TT772.B75 2010
746.44--dc22   2009047430

Ingram 4/10 42334
32.99

In-house editor: Nancy Breen

Designer: Julie Barnett

Production coordinator: Greg Nock

Photographers: Al Parrish, Bethany Tozer

Stylist: Jan Nickum

ACKNOWLEDGEMENTS

This book is the result of many people joining forces to breathe new life into old embroidery designs. Thanks to Jay Fishman of Wicked Stitch of the West for working tirelessly with me on the digitized motifs; to Missy Shepler for redrawing a hundred iron-on transfers; and to Nancy Breen for all she did to shape the project.

Special thanks are due to the companies that have supplied materials for the projects in these pages. Please take a moment to check the list of resources at the back of the book, and use these wonderful products when you can. In particular, Brother International, MidSouth's Best Sewing and Floriani Products/RNK Distributing provide a level of ongoing support that makes my work possible—and enjoyable.

As always, my family and friends have been great supporters, cheerleaders and fans. Patricia and Jonathan, Mom and Dad, Linda and Pauline, and many others—you know who you are—thank you!

The WORKBASKET® was born in October 1935, and in contemplating contemporaneous events, I celebrate one particularly important to me: Happy birthday, Mom.

Whenever I write about advances in embroidery, I think of my great-grandmother, Maggie Kemp, and my grandfather, Foster Jackson. Papa gave me a tiny embroidery kit—essentially a penny square plus needle, thread and hoop—when I was very young, and I remember that as my first exposure to embroidery. Maggie owned the first sewing machine I ever saw that did more than make straight stitches, and she made me a dress with scallops machine-embroidered on the collar (see photo below). I would dearly love to show them the machines I work with today!

table *of* contents

INTRODUCTION

The designs in these pages have been chosen from six decades of a little magazine called *The WORKBASKET*. Aimed at homemakers (in the days when the word had no pejorative connotations), *The WORKBASKET* presented designs for needlework and other crafts in its pages, often in the form of iron-on transfers. The artistic styles vary widely over the years, with some motifs instantly recognizable as a product of mid-twentieth century America and others decidedly more modern.

While there are still many hand embroiderers in the twenty-first century, the last three decades have brought a marvelous innovation: embroidery machines for the home user. These technological marvels can stitch a design in a fraction of the time required for hand embroidery. What's more, machine embroidery can be programmed to mimic the appearance of hand-embroidered heirlooms.

Redwork from The WORKBASKET happily straddles the fence between old and new as it presents one hundred designs culled from thousands that appeared in *The WORKBASKET* magazine. These designs are offered in formats for both machine and hand embroiderers.

In these pages, you'll find basic information for stitching redwork designs with the method of your choice. If you're seeking more detailed basic information, refer to *Resources* (page 124) for suggestions for further reading.

Enjoy your foray into old/new redwork. Have fun!

A Brief History of Redwork

We take the hundreds of thread colors in our modern workbaskets for granted, but plentiful, inexpensive and colorfast dyes are a relatively recent innovation.

DEVELOPING RED THREAD

Europeans during the Renaissance knew that madder root could be used to dye textiles red, but the results were often an unsatisfactory shade of orange or coral. Only dyers in the Ottoman Empire and India seemed to possess the key to consistent red dyes.

In the eighteenth century, French entrepreneurs finally unlocked the secret of vibrant Turkey Red, named for the Ottoman dyers who first introduced the color to Europe. Their discovery, coupled with imports of cotton from British outposts in India, made inexpensive red cotton threads and flosses available to those who couldn't afford silk or woolen threads. Best of all, the new red dye produced thread that held its color even through harsh laundering.

By the mid-nineteenth century, red embroidery was everywhere. Common laundry marks, intended simply to distinguish one person's linens from another's, went from small white-on-white stitches to elaborately embellished monograms in fiery red. Table linens, dishtowels and handkerchiefs, subject to everyday use and rigorous laundering, now could be decorated with colored motifs. Cotton threads were less expensive than silk, so many more households could afford to embellish fabrics and clothing.

By the end of the nineteenth century, commercial dyeing and the development of synthetic dyes encompassed a wide spectrum of colors that could be reliably and consistently reproduced. Cotton was readily available around the world, and embroidery floss in many colors became a sewing box staple.

Various Threads and Shades of Red
Modern machine and hand embroiderers have a vast array of threads and hues to choose from.
Threads by DMC, Kreinik Manufacturing Co., Inc., Sulky of America, Weeks Dye Works and YLI.

THE POPULARITY OF REDWORK

The embroidery style we know as redwork reached the peak of its popularity during the nineteenth and early twentieth centuries. Only a few simple stitches are needed to create redwork embroideries, and their outline-only design style shortens the working time dramatically. Redwork is both simple enough for children and beginners and enjoyable enough for more advanced stitchers.

In the past, redwork designs printed on muslin and known as penny squares were available at general stores along with the floss and needles necessary for embroidery. Many children learned to stitch with these simple materials.

Women were also able to stamp their own designs at home, transferring patterns to parchment paper with a piercing tool and stamping powder. They were even encouraged to begin home-based businesses stamping redwork designs on fabric for sale.

Iron-on transfers developed in the 1870s were a great improvement over the cumbersome stamping technique. Magazines offered transfers as an incentive for subscribers, and catalogs offered patterns, fabrics, needles and threads for redwork.

REDWORK NOW

Today, redwork is a general term signifying outline-only embroidery stitched primarily with a single color of cotton thread, using outline stitch (also called stem stitch) and a handful of other embroidery stitches. The designs can be stitched in any color and are sometimes given such names as bluework, greenwork or "redwork in purple." The unifying characteristic of redwork embroidery is the pleasing contrast between the colored thread and the plain woven ground, usually muslin or other cotton fabric.

Redwork faded in popularity by the middle of the twentieth century, but it never disappeared completely. As years went by, redwork quilts and other linens became targets for antique hunters as buyers discovered the monochromatic designs' continuing appeal. Now that the "retro" look is trendy, redwork motifs are back in the spotlight.

With the advent of computerized embroidery machines for the home, redwork embroidery has entered a new phase. By programming the motif in digitizing software, a stitcher can embellish almost any textile in a matter of minutes. Redwork designs have always been quick to stitch, but each machine embroidery motif included with this book can be completed in less than ten minutes!

More Than Red-on-White
Redwork needn't be red, and vivid color on a black ground makes an especially dramatic alternative. *Design: #MSC047. Thread is Coats & Clark Color Twist; fabric by Charles Craft.*

THE WORKBASKET MAGAZINE

In October 1935, the Detroit Tigers won the World Series, besting the Chicago Cubs four games to two. The Italian Army invaded Ethiopia, and Germany began its buildup to World War II. On the domestic front, the Depression continued and the unemployment rate was over twenty percent. A DuPont chemist produced the first completely synthetic fiber, nylon, and Benny Goodman gave birth to Swing. A loaf of bread cost eight cents, hamburger was eleven cents a pound and a gallon of gasoline cost just a dime.

Sometime during October 1935, John and Clara Tillotson sat at their kitchen table and produced the first issue of a monthly magazine they called *Aunt Martha's Workbasket: Home and Needlecraft, For Pleasure and Profit*. In those sixteen newsprint pages, the Tillotsons offered readers a compilation of patterns and a promise to return with future issues. The original price was fifteen cents per issue, or one dollar for a year-long subscription.

For the next sixty-one years, *The WORKBASKET* published regular issues filled with patterns for embroidery, knitting, crochet, quilting and other handicrafts. While the first few issues were essentially advertising brochures for patterns available via mail order, most included a quilt block design and a sheet of transfers for embroidery. *Aunt Martha's* was dropped from the title in 1942, and the subhead followed in 1959.

THE WORKBASKET GROWS

The Tillotsons sold individual patterns as well as their magazine. The patterns carried the *Aunt Martha's* name and cost ten cents. Occasionally a bundle of patterns was released in magazine format, eventually becoming *The WORKBASKET*. In 1949, the pattern company and

**Vintage Copies
of *The WORKBASKET***

magazine publisher separated when the Tillotsons sold the *Aunt Martha's* name, now a part of Colonial Patterns, Inc., and formed a magazine publishing house called Modern Handcraft.

Over the years, *The WORKBASKET* included feature articles about the benefits, financial and otherwise, of crafting to women and households. Columns included cooking tips and brief craft ideas called "Making Cents." The focus was on providing women with means to earn pin money during the decades when few worked outside the home. The projects, designs and instructions were a constant part of the magazine, varying in style as American culture changed, but always focused on creativity and the home.

CHANGING WITH AMERICA

Advertisements and prices in *The WORKBASKET*, as well as the style of its projects and embroidery designs, trace a road map of the changes in America from the 1930s to the 1990s. The earliest issues were published when many people were jobless and the "make do or do without" attitude was prevalent. Home-based handicrafts served a practical purpose as well as providing a creative outlet.

In the 1950s and 1960s, the United States experienced its post-war boom. While more households could afford to purchase rather than make necessary items, those who had matured during the Depression and war years still exercised creative frugality at home. By 1966, *The WORKBASKET*'s cover price had risen to twenty-five cents. The hippie culture of the 1960s and 1970s brought crafts renewed popularity as young people embroidered their denim jeans, wove belts and headbands and tied macramé plant holders. *The WORKBASKET* kept pace again, and by 1975 was charging thirty-five cents per copy.

1980S TO TODAY

In the 1980s and 1990s, there were still plenty of readers interested in *The WORKBASKET*'s traditional patterns and ideas. A new use for designs and transfers emerged as fabric paints became popular, and many crafters began painting t-shirts and tote bags. By this time, *The WORKBASKET* was published in full color on quality paper, although it retained its diminutive size.

More than half a century after the first issue was released, *The WORKBASKET* was still being published by Modern Handcraft. A ten-issue subscription cost six dollars.

In 1990, the company welcomed a new owner and reinvented itself as a thoroughly modern magazine publisher. *The WORKBASKET* and two other bimonthly titles were still published, but with upgraded content and higher prices. In 1992, the $2.95 cover price reflected decades of economic growth and inflation. At its peak in the mid-nineties, *The WORKBASKET* produced 280 pages annually for 800,000 readers.

The last issue of *The WORKBASKET* was published in 1996, when Krause Publications purchased the rights to the magazine and merged its content into *Flower & Gardens Craft*, which later became *Great American Crafts*. In 2001, the name changed again, to *Michael's Create!*

The WORKBASKET's embroidery transfers became collector's items; both the transfers and the magazine itself can be found in antique malls, flea markets and estate sales and through online auctions. The designs vary from timeless folk art motifs to retro animated china to sleek sports cars. While some designs are too dated to use, others are as fresh and fun as the day they were published. Still others provoke nostalgic smiles or memories of grandmother's shady guest room with hand-embroidered pillowcases on the welcoming bed.

CONTENT FOR A NEW AGE

This book includes a CD-ROM with 100 embroidery designs culled from six decades of *The WORKBASKET*. The original transfers have been redrawn but not altered, to provide high quality line art that is faithful to the originals for twenty-first century embroiderers. In addition, the designs have been digitized for embroidery on computerized machines. The technology has changed since 1935, but not the enjoyment and satisfaction of embroidering, stitching and creating.

FABRICS AND BLANKS

The most traditional fabric for redwork embroidery is muslin. It has a smooth texture that shows the embroidery stitches to advantage, and is inexpensive and readily available. Choose bleached white muslin for a crisp, fresh appearance, or unbleached muslin for an aged patina and rustic look.

Other fabrics also lend themselves to outline-only embroidery. Linen and denim are two basic choices, but consider taffeta, satin, and moiré fabrics as more dramatic backgrounds for redwork. In general, choose a smooth plain-weave fabric, not one with a nap or pile that will swallow the stitches; but textured fabrics such as moderately coarse linen and silk dupioni make good backgrounds for embroidery. Solid-color fabrics are preferable to prints, as they provide better contrast for the embroidery design.

One advantage to machine-embroidered redwork is the ability to stitch on knits as well as stable woven fabrics. Stabilizers applied to the knit fabric render it firm enough for stitching, and the cut-away varieties can be left in place behind the embroidery to provide continuing support during wear and care.

Blanks, finished items with space for embroidery, also provide perfect platforms for redwork. Pillowcases and dishtowels come readily to mind, but consider also aprons, t-shirts, sweatshirts and afghans.

> ### More On Blanks
>
> For more on finding and using blanks, see my book *Fill in the Blanks with Machine Embroidery* (Rebecca Kemp Brent, Krause Publications, 2007).

Machine-Embroidered Redwork on Dress Blank
Personalize blanks with charming redwork motifs in machine or hand embroidery. *Designs: # ANI035 and #ANI032. Dress from All About Blanks.*

Find blanks by shopping at local retailers or by searching the Internet for suppliers. Specialty blanks retailers carry a surprising array of ready-to-stitch items, including heirloom dresses and accessories for children and adults. Hand needleworkers may find usable blanks at machine embroidery Web sites, while machine embroiderers may be surprised to find blanks for their embroidery through hand needlework vendors.

Consider unusual blanks as well, such as clocks (remove the plastic cover, disassemble the hands and insert an embroidered fabric face before reassembling the clock), wooden boxes (create a fabric cover for the box lid, or machine embroider directly on balsa wood and attach it to the box with glue), and lotion dispensers (specially made to accommodate an embroidered fabric panel).

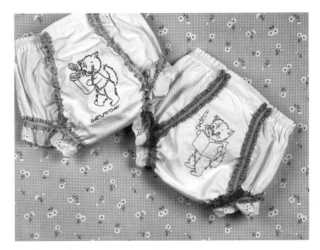

Dressed-Up Diaper Covers
What could be cuter than blank diaper covers embroidered with days-of-the-week cats? *Designs: #DOW007 and #DOW001. Diaper covers from All About Blanks.*

Caring for Redwork

The original redwork craze was sparked by the arrival of colorfast red thread on the market, so it's ironic that colorfastness is still an issue with today's embroiderers. Although some red fabrics and threads are marked colorfast, it's important to follow the manufacturer's instructions for care.

To test an unknown textile for colorfastness, dampen the fabric or thread with warm water and rub it against a piece of white cotton. If the color transfers to the cotton, the colored material should be pre-treated to preserve its color.

With the high contrast between a pale background and dark thread that characterizes redwork, it may be especially prudent to pre-treat materials for a project. Some sources recommend washing red and other dark, rich colors with vinegar and/or salt to set the color, while others contend that vinegar and salt don't contribute to colorfastness. A commercial product called Retayne is available to help set the color of commercially dyed textiles, and because its application can be controlled by following the manufacturer's instructions, Retayne yields consistently satisfactory results.

Most fabrics can be machine washed and dried before beginning a project, but threads should be washed by hand to prevent tangling. Remove the paper bands from a skein of floss and tie white thread or string around the skein at one or two points. Submerge it in a pan of warm water with Retayne (follow the manufacturer's instructions for amount) or a little vinegar and agitate the thread gently. Rinse the skein and roll it in a towel, squeezing to remove excess moisture. Lay the thread on a dry towel and allow it to air dry.

If the color in a finished project does run, don't despair. A detergent called Synthrapol, manufactured for dyers, is specially formulated to suspend stray particles of dye in the wash water without redepositing the dye on the textile. Repeated washings may be necessary, but Synthrapol can remove unsightly color runs and save a damaged project.

THREADS

Machine Embroidery Threads
Threads shown are by Coats & Clark, DMC, Floriani, Sulky of America, Weeks Dye Works and YLI.

Using a single color of thread to create an image is the essence of redwork embroidery. The default thread for machine embroidery is 40-weight rayon or polyester, while the usual thread for hand-embroidered redwork is six-strand cotton embroidery floss. However, embroiderers today have a wealth of readily available threads from which to choose.

MACHINE EMBROIDERY THREADS

40-WEIGHT POLYESTER OR RAYON
The default embroidery thread and weight, both fibers are manufactured with the lovely sheen of silk. The designs on the CD-ROM accompanying this book are digitized for this thread weight.

MATTE-FINISH THREADS
For machine embroidery that more closely resembles hand embroidery, look for threads with a non-shiny (matte) finish. Size 50 cotton machine embroidery thread and polyester thread textured to look like cotton will work well with the designs on the CD-ROM.

30-WEIGHT RAYON
OR COTTON EMBROIDERY THREAD
This heavier weight thread can be used for the redwork designs. It works best in designs having few details or small stitches, and yields a heavier line of embroidery.

ALL-PURPOSE POLYESTER SEWING THREAD
This thread easily crosses the line between function and fashion. The strength of polyester and the sewing thread's matte finish are a winning combination for machine embroidery that resembles work done by hand. Choose a quality sewing thread with low lint for best results.

SPECIALTY THREADS
Look for variegated, tweedy, color twisted, glow-in-the-dark and metallic machine embroidery threads to add extra interest to redwork motifs.

What About Heavy Threads?

The machine embroidery designs on the book's CD-ROM are digitized for 40-weight embroidery thread and others with similar weight and hand. The appearance of multiple strands found in hand embroidery is duplicated by passing over each stitch more than once. In addition, the complexity of some motifs necessitates tiny stitches placed close together.

Those characteristics render most of these designs unsuitable for heavyweight threads such as 12-weight cotton or wool-blend machine embroidery thread. If you choose to experiment with a heavier-than-usual thread, work a sample first on scrap fabric and proceed with caution.

BOBBIN THREADS

Machine embroiderers must also consider thread to fill the bobbin. Regular embroidery bobbin thread, generally finer than the thread used in the needle, works well for redwork motifs. It is also possible to fill the bobbin with the same thread used in the needle. The latter approach is especially suitable when the wrong side of the embroidery will be visible, as on a dishtowel or other single-layer blank, resulting in an almost reversible motif.

Key to Stitched Out Machine Embroidery Threads

Sulky, 40-wt. rayon

Sulky, 40-wt. rayon variegated

Coats & Clark, polyester machine embroidery

Coats & Clark, Dual Duty XP® All Purpose

DMC, 50-wt. cotton

Sulky, 30-wt. cotton Blendables

Weeks Dye Works, 40-wt. Sewing Thread

YLI, Fusions

YLI, Colours

YLI, 50-wt. silk

Floriani, metallic

Hand Embroidery Threads
Threads shown are by DMC and
Kreinik Manufacturing Co., Inc.

HAND EMBROIDERY THREADS

SIX-STRAND COTTON EMBROIDERY FLOSS
Not only is this the historical choice for redwork, six-strand floss is also the most familiar thread for hand embroidery. The floss separates easily into six individual plies. Cut a working length of floss, separate the required number of strands (two or three for most redwork) individually from the floss, and thread the plies together into the eye of an embroidery needle.

SPECIALTY FLOSSES
Six-strand floss is also available in variegated skeins that cover a range of shades within one color family. Hand-dyed and overdyed flosses are similar to variegated threads, but have more subtle, irregular, and intriguing color variation. Metallic, glow-in-the-dark, and satin-finish flosses are used like cotton floss, but give embroidery an extra something. These specialty threads are wonderful in simple, single-color redwork motifs.

PEARL COTTON
This non-separable embroidery cotton comes in a variety of sizes. Size 8 or 12 pearl cotton (also called cotton perlé) can be used for redwork embroidery.

SILK THREADS
Luxurious silk thread is available as stranded floss or twisted thread similar to pearl cotton. Look for variegated and hand-dyed silk threads, too.

WOOL EMBROIDERY YARN

Usually associated with crewel embroidery, wool yarns can also be stitched into redwork projects. Consider especially how woolen embroidery can accent a sweater or felted item. Keep in mind that while heavy wool threads may be too large for detailed redwork motifs, the designs can be enlarged to accommodate fatter threads.

BLENDING FILAMENTS AND BRAIDS

Blending filament is a fine single strand that is threaded through the needle along with the embroidery thread. It adds a subtle sparkle to the embroidery stitches. Braids are available in a variety of sizes, some of which are too heavy for redwork, but consider the finest braids for special redwork designs.

Redwork Style with Color
Hand-embroidered redwork can be stitched in several colors rather than the traditional single hue. The top pillowcase was stitched with two strands of DMC Variations floss #4240 (blue), #4045 (green) and #4075 (yellow); the bottom pillowcase was stitched with two strands of Weeks Dye Works floss #2113 (Union Blue), #2198 (Ivy) and #2224 (Squash). *Design: #FLW094. Pillowcases embroidered by Nancy Breen.*

Key to Stitched Out Hand Embroidery Threads

Weeks Dye Works, Turkish Red cotton floss (2 strands)

DMC, 6-strand cotton floss (2 strands)

DMC, No. 12 pearl cotton

Kreinik, Silk Mori

Kreinik, Silk Serica

Kreinik, Silk Bella

DMC, Jewels metallic

Kreinik, #4 braid

Kreinik, #8 braid

Kreinik, Cord

Kreinik, Blending Filament

NOVEL IDEAS FOR REDWORK

As beautiful as traditional one-color redwork on a light background is, these simple motifs can be used in other ways as well.

COLOR WORK

Why stop with red thread? Stitch these designs in any color to match personal taste, décor or mood.

Select a black background fabric and neon thread for a vibrant design. Work with tea-dyed muslin and muted, overdyed floss for a country palette. Use matching thread and fabric colors for highly sophisticated tone-on-tone embroidery even suitable for formal occasions.

Threads That Change Hues
Design #HOM078 machine-embroidered in variegated thread. *Thread by Madeira.*

VARIEGATED AND MULTICOLOR THREADS

Experiment with variegated thread, which combines several tints and shades of one color, and multicolored thread that contains short lengths of several different hues. These threads vary greatly from one brand to another, especially in the length of thread between color changes.

Stitch the motif first on a fabric scrap to gauge the effect of a particular thread. Redwork is unlikely to develop stripes as filled designs can when stitched with variegated threads, but check first to determine whether the thread variations cause parts of the design to fade into the background.

Blue on Blue
Design #NOS056 machine-embroidered in dark blue thread against a blue background. *Thread: Fusions by YLI; fabric by DMC.*

QUILTING

Redwork motifs, especially those with the simplest shapes and fewest details, can be used as quilting designs, whether stitched by hand or machine.

For hand embroidery, transfer the design to a plain block within the quilt, layer the quilt sandwich, and sew the redwork design with quilting stitches as usual.

Size 12 pearl cotton is a great thread for quilting redwork designs, as it emphasizes the design more than a finer thread can.

Machine embroiderers can quilt with redwork by layering and basting the quilt, then positioning the hoop as desired and stitching redwork motifs through all the quilt layers. Quilt-as-you-go techniques that break the quilt into smaller sections for quilting are ideal for machine embroidered quilting, as the sections are easier to handle and less likely to create drag and distortion as the embroidery progresses.

Quilting Redwork Designs
Design #FRV020 used as a quilting motif.

COLORING FUN

Create a textile coloring book with redwork outlines stitched with black thread. Use textile markers or dyes to color the motifs. Choose fabric crayons, paints or markers, and follow the manufacturer's instructions to set the color on the fabric.

Many artist colors can also be used on fabric. Redwork that will be framed or otherwise used without laundering can be colored with almost any pigment. Experiment first on a fabric scrap to be sure the color won't bleed or feather into the fabric weave.

Fabric can be colored with artist's pastels, oil paint sticks and even ordinary crayons. When the coloring is complete, sandwich the project between layers of paper towels and press with a warm or hot iron to remove excess

---

wax and set the color. Some of these media can withstand washing, but the colors may fade. Always test the chosen media and fabric first to avoid unpleasant surprises later.

Even projects that will be washed can be colored with such unexpected media as watercolor pencils and crayons. Allow the tinted redwork to dry, then paint it with a coat of textile medium, a sealant available in art supply departments or with dyeing and fabric painting supplies. The textile medium covers and protects the colors through gentle hand washing.

Unique Gift
Stitch a redwork design or two on a child's t-shirt and wrap with a box of fabric crayons for an interactive gift. Include washable markers instead and the child can wash and recolor over and over!
Design: #JUV072. Crayons by Pentel Arts.

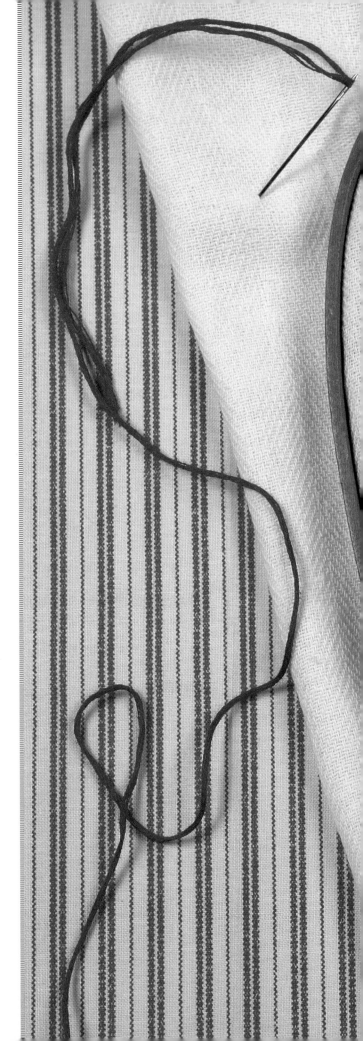

working *the* designs

Traditional redwork requires very few supplies: embroidery floss, fabric, needle and hoop. With the variety of materials available to the twenty-first century crafter, the choices broaden to include a wealth of fabrics, threads and supplies.

What follows is an overview of the materials and techniques for both machine and hand embroidery.

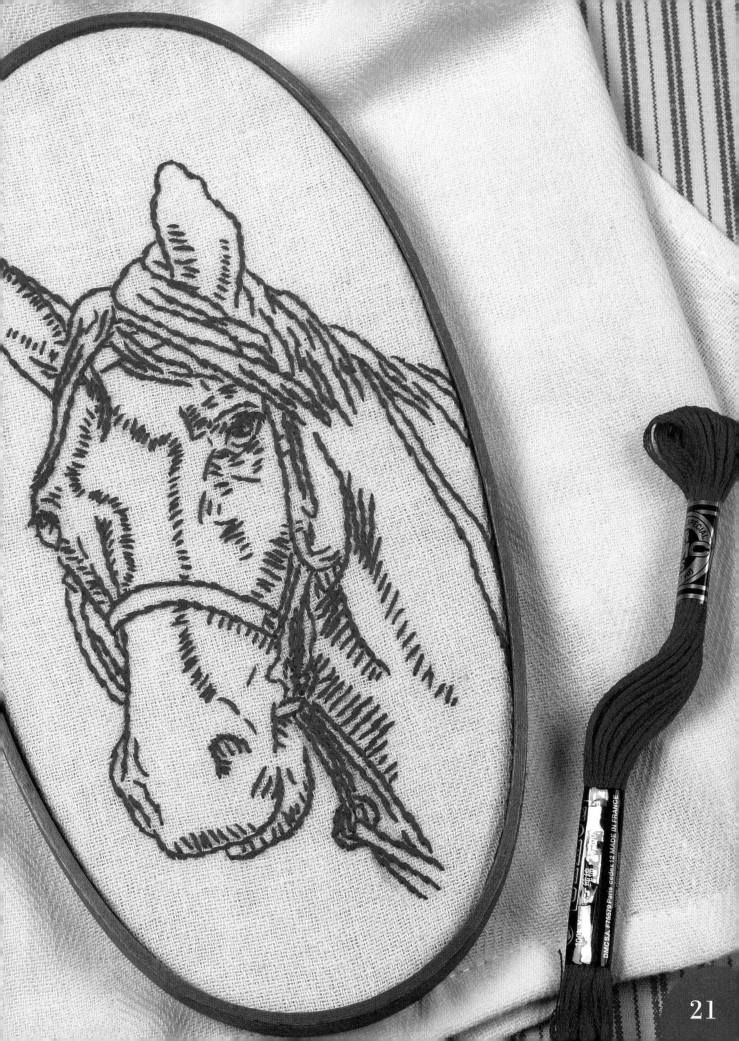

Machine-Embroidered Redwork

Machine-embroidered redwork has two great advantages over its hand-worked counterpart: its speed and the ability to stitch on virtually any fabric. In addition, there is no need to transfer patterns to the fabric, which is particularly important when the fabric is a dark color or too delicate for marking. Repeating designs are simple with machine embroidery, which can tirelessly produce exact duplicates of a motif over and over again.

Fabric and thread are the main components of machine-embroidered redwork, as they are for hand embroidery. In addition, machine embroiderers need stabilizers and marking tools to achieve the best results.

Changing Design Size

Redwork designs can be scaled up or down with embroidery machine controls or customizing software. Enlarging or reducing the design without changing the stitch count, or density, will also lengthen or shorten individual stitches within the design. Enlarging or decreasing by more than twenty percent without altering the stitch count may yield unsatisfactory results, although it can be an effective strategy if the design will be stitched with a heavier or lighter than usual thread.

Resizing software will automatically recalculate the number of stitches in the resized design and is recommended for changes greater than twenty percent. A motif resized in this way will cover the fabric as effectively at the new size as at the original dimensions, provided the same thread weight is used.

stabilizers

Stabilizers for machine embroidery fall into two general categories: removable and permanent. Removable stabilizers include tear-away products, water- and heat-soluble stabilizers and liquids applied to fabric. Cut-away stabilizers are permanent and remain behind the embroidery throughout the life of the project.

CHOOSING A STABILIZER

When determining which stabilizer is best suited for an embroidery design, consider the fabric that will be embroidered and the character of the design itself. Stable fabrics generally require less stabilizer than loosely woven or stretchy materials, so removable stabilizers work well with most stable fabrics. In contrast, knits and fabrics with stretch or unsteady construction need the continuing support that cut-away stabilizers provide.

Embroidery designs with high stitch density and large areas of fill need more stabilization than openwork and outline-only motifs. Because redwork falls into the latter category, redwork machine embroidery generally requires less stabilizer than a filled motif of comparable size.

Combining the two considerations (fabric type and stitch density), redwork on a stable fabric such as traditional muslin or plain-weave cotton requires little stabilizer, and choices from the removable category are most appropriate. That leaves machine embroiderers to choose among tear-away, water- and heat-soluble, and liquid stabilizers by considering the project itself and its projected use and care.

TEAR-AWAY STABILIZER

Tear-away stabilizer provides excellent stability for machine embroidered redwork. The tear-away can be hooped along with the fabric, or an adhesive tear-away stabilizer can be used for embroidery without hooping the fabric (see *Hooping Strategies*, page 26).

The drawback to tear-away stabilizer for redwork is the difficulty of removing bits and pieces of stabilizer when the design is complete. This is particularly problematic when the embroidery design is finely detailed, with many lines of stitches surrounding small areas of fabric and stabilizer. Remaining bits of stabilizer make the embroidery wrong side rough, and they may shadow through the ground fabric to be visible from the right side.

Using traditional tear-away stabilizer on projects that will be lined or in which the wrong side of the embroidery will be covered minimizes the disadvantages. Tear-away wash-away stabilizer, which dissolves into a web of fibers when washed, is another solution. However, water- and heat-soluble stabilizers can be even more effective, as they can be completely removed after embroidery from even the tiniest negative spaces in the design.

A Variety of Stabilizers
Fabric type and stitch density are considerations when choosing the right stabilizer. The above photo includes iron-on tear-away, cut-away mesh, adhesive water-soluble, tear-away and water-soluble stabilizers. *Stabilizers pictured are by Floriani.*

Good and Bad Stitch Registration

If insufficient stabilizer is used, the design may not stitch accurately over previous stitches, leading to poor design registration, as shown in the lower photo. *Design: #MSC043.*

SOLUBLE STABILIZERS

Some water-soluble stabilizers resemble plastic wrap. These stabilizer films are available in several weights, any of which may provide enough support for redwork; however, water-soluble films can stretch during hooping and embroidery. Other water-soluble stabilizers resemble a lightweight nonwoven fabric; these provide firm support and are unlikely to stretch.

Heat-soluble stabilizers work much like water-solubles but can be used with nonwashable fabrics. Be sure to read and follow manufacturer's instructions for any soluble stabilizer, and use the recommended water or iron temperature for easiest stabilizer removal.

LIQUID STABILIZERS

The third category of removable stabilizers is liquids. This includes paint-on and spray fabric stabilizers, as well as humble laundry starch. Like water-soluble stabilizers, liquids are appropriate only for fabrics and projects that can be washed.

Paint-on stabilizer can be made at home by saving scraps of water-soluble stabilizer from other projects and dissolving them in water. Refrigerate the mixture in a spray bottle or covered jar to prevent spoilage. Apply the stabilizer generously and allow the fabric to air dry; the result is a stiff, papery texture.

Fabric stabilizer and spray starch are both available in aerosol cans. Apply them in a series of light coats to the fabric wrong side, pressing with a warm iron between coats. For best results, allow the starchy liquid a moment to penetrate the fabric before pressing. Either regular or heavy spray starch can be used. Starch works best on absorbent natural-fiber fabrics such as cotton and linen.

Starch alone will not always provide sufficient stability for embroidery. However, with the low stitch counts of the redwork designs in this book, you may need only starch for embroidery on stable woven fabrics. Always stitch a sample first to be sure the starch provides perfect stitch-outs with your hoop, machine and fabric choices.

PERMANENT STABILIZERS AND KNITS

Permanent stabilizers are needed, even with redwork designs, when motifs are stitched on knit fabrics, including sweatshirts and t-shirts. To stabilize these materials, choose an iron-on or adhesive cut-away stabilizer. Attach it to the fabric or garment wrong side according to the manufacturer's instructions, then hoop the stabilized fabric. When the embroidery is complete, carefully trim away the excess stabilizer, leaving a small margin around the embroidered motif. The stabilizer remains in place to support the design, preventing unsightly puckers and pulling.

Getting Rid of Ridges

If the trimmed stabilizer edge creates a visible ridge on the right side of the fabric, use pinking shears to trim the stabilizer. The jagged edge is more likely to blend seamlessly into the fabric.

---

marking tools

Machine embroidery requires minimal marking to pinpoint the embroidery location; however, the marks usually will not be covered by redwork, so removability is crucial. Always test the chosen tool on a fabric scrap to guarantee that its marks can be removed without damaging the project.

To position the design, mark the motif's horizontal and vertical axes by drawing two perpendicular lines that intersect at the center point or by making smaller hash marks where the axes intersect each other and the hoop perimeter. Use these marks to place the fabric squarely in the hoop, and use the machine's controls to position the needle precisely over the center mark before embroidering.

Since fine lines are more accurate, use a marking tool with a fine or renewable point or an edge that can be sharpened.

Here are some marking tools to consider:

Water- or air-soluble markers. Simple to use and remove, these provide consistently visible results.

Use air-soluble markers when water could damage the project, but be aware that the long-term effects of marker chemicals on fabrics is unknown. These markers may be fine for quick projects, but choose another method for heirlooms intended to stand the test of time. Items marked with an air-soluble pen should be hooped quickly, as the marks may begin to disappear right away.

Water-soluble markers are a popular choice. Keep a spray bottle or a water-primed foam paintbrush at hand to remove the marks before ironing. Water-soluble markers may ultimately damage fabric, too, so use plenty of clear water (no detergent or soap) to remove the marks thoroughly after embroidering.

Tailor's chalk. If water might damage the project, use a powdery chalk that can be brushed away. Another appropriate formulation can be removed with a burst of steam from an iron. Work with a chalk color close to the fabric hue to minimize the impact of any chalk residue.

Stickers. Stickers are wonderful for temporarily marking the design center point, and they guarantee that no marks remain on the fabric when the project is

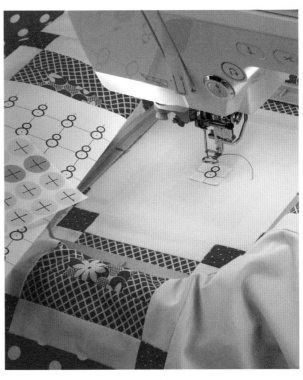

Sticker Marks the Needle Position
Stickers supplied with the machine or created at home can be used to mark design locations on difficult fabrics.

complete. Mark a cross (+) on a small, round sticker, position it at the desired location and center the needle over the cross. Remember to remove the sticker before sewing. Some embroidery machines can actually read special stickers to position the embroidery design precisely at the desired location, even rotating the motif to compensate for hooping deviations!

Computer-printed templates. Templates created in embroidery software and printed from a computer are ideal when exact placement of motifs is crucial (e.g., when combining motifs for a continuous border). Printable, self-adhesive, semi-transparent template paper (such as Floriani Template Tearaway) creates reusable templates with enough transparency to reveal adjacent motifs or background fabric details.

Marking the horizontal and vertical axes on the template means no placement marks to erase from the fabric. Leave the template in place during hooping and positioning the needle, but remember to remove the template before stitching.

hooping strategies

The most reliable hooping strategy for redwork, like any embroidery, is to use the smallest possible hoop, stabilize the fabric properly, and hoop the fabric securely. Exceptions can and sometimes should be made to accommodate specialty fabrics or unusual situations, such as the examples that follow.

If a delicate fabric such as silk organza or dupioni is used for the redwork embroidery, hooping may cause tearing or bruising. Instead, hoop an adhesive stabilizer and attach the fabric to the stabilizer, laying the fabric atop the hoop.

Adhesive stabilizers may be water-activated or paper-release. For the former, apply plain water lightly to the hooped stabilizer; too much water makes removing the embroidered fabric difficult. For paper-release stabilizers, hoop the stabilizer with the paper covering intact, then score and remove the paper from the area inside the hoop. Attach the fabric to the stabilizer, centering the design location, and stitch.

To stabilize a knit fabric for redwork, back it with iron-on stabilizer. Hoop the stabilized fabric directly, or hoop adhesive stabilizer and attach the stabilized knit to it.

Adhesive stabilizers are also available in water-soluble formulations. If the redwork project is water-friendly, water-soluble adhesive stabilizer is the perfect answer for difficult hooping situations.

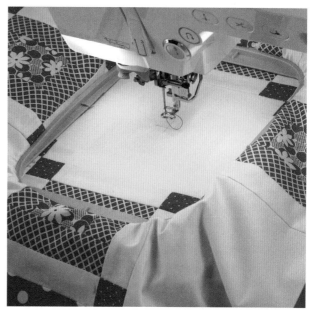

Construction First
Sewing pieces together before starting embroidering both fills the hoop completely and creates a larger area for embroidery.

Another situation that calls for special hooping is embroidery on ready-made items, also called blanks. To stitch close to an edge or embroider an item too small to hoop, attach strips of iron-on tear-away stabilizer or scrap fabric, basted in place, to the edges of the small item, increasing its size to fill the hoop. Another strategy that works for both small and bulky items (for example, those with thick seam allowances near the embroidery area) is hooping adhesive stabilizer as directed above.

What Does "Smallest Possible Hoop" Mean?

As machine hoops have gotten larger, it's fun to create large designs by combining smaller motifs, or to hoop once and stitch several designs in a single embroidery field. However, as hoop size increases, stability can suffer. This is often seen near the middle of a hoop's longest side, when fabric shifts slightly during embroidery and the outline, stitched last, is thrown off. Even redwork designs can be affected by fabric shifts when the needle returns to stitch over early stitches just before completing the design, and fabric shifting is most likely to occur with the lightweight fabrics favored for traditional redwork.

To combat fabric slippage, use the smallest hoop that will hold the embroidery design. For most of the redwork designs on the book's CD-ROM, that will be the standard 4" × 4" (100mm × 100mm) hoop; for others, a 5" × 7" (130mm × 180mm) hoop is required.

HAND-EMBROIDERED REDWORK

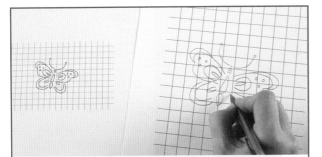

Resizing with a Grid
Use a grid to enlarge or reduce a design without the use of a photocopier or computer.

Changing Design Size

Redwork designs can be scaled up or down in size. Before changing a design's size, look at the complexity of the drawing and decide whether scaling down will pack the details too closely, or whether a simple motif will become too bare if enlarged.

The simplest way to change the size of a design is to use a photocopier that can make the change automatically. A printer or scanner connected to a computer may also be able to enlarge or reduce a motif. In either case, choose the new size by specifying a percentage of the existing design's size or by selecting from a list of predetermined options. Graphics software is another option for changing motif sizes.

If a photocopier or software is unavailable, use a measured grid to alter the design size. For example, to double the size of a motif, draw a grid of lines ¼" (6mm) apart over the existing motif. On a blank sheet of paper, draw a grid with the same number of cells as the original, this time with lines ½" (1.3cm) apart. Copy the design one square at a time into the larger grid to make the enlargement. To decrease the design size, make the new grid with lines more closely spaced than the original.

Hand embroidery has an enduring popularity not eroded by modern alternatives. Hand embroiderers enjoy the tranquility and sense of purposeful creativity that stitching with needle and thread provides. Handwork is portable and as varied as the stitchers themselves, and redwork is especially appealing with its minimal material requirements. Just grab a needle, thread, fabric and hoop and enjoy stitching almost anywhere, indoors or out.

NEEDLE KNOW-HOW

Because redwork is usually stitched with multiple plies of cotton embroidery floss, it is important to have a needle with an eye large enough for more than one strand. Embroidery needles (also called crewel needles) have sharpened points to pierce the background fabric and large eyes to accommodate thicker threads. Chenille needles are another option, with even larger eyes that can accept strands of wool or specialty fibers.

transferring designs

Before stitching begins, the redwork design must be reproduced on the fabric itself. Several methods are available; choose one that works well for the project fabric, considering factors such as visibility and specific care requirements. In general, use a light blue, gray or red line on light-colored fabrics and a white or yellow line on darks.

For many transfer methods, applying spray starch to the fabric makes transferring easier. The starch locks the fabric grain and stiffens the material to eliminate distortion as the marking tool drags across the fabric.

If spray starch is inappropriate, stabilize the fabric with freezer paper before transferring the design. Place the fabric face down on the ironing board and cover it with a piece of freezer paper, shiny side down. Press firmly with a warm iron. The freezer paper bonds temporarily to the fabric, making a sturdy surface for tracing the design. Remove the freezer paper before stitching.

DIRECT TRACING METHOD

The most basic method of transferring designs to fabric is direct tracing. It is suitable for light-colored light- to medium-weight fabrics.

Begin by printing the chosen design on plain white paper from the graphics files on the CD-ROM included with this book. Tape the design to a light table or a sunny window pane and cover it with the project fabric. The design will be visible through the fabric.

Use a hard lead pencil, a water- or air-soluble marker or a sharpened chalk pencil to trace the design lines onto the fabric.

Results on Different Fabrics
From upper right, clockwise: water-soluble pen on dark and light fabrics; white chalk pencil on dark fabric; red iron-on transfer pen on light fabric; and red transfer pen on paper, ready to be ironed onto fabric. *Design: #FLOW095.*

Using a Light Table

Taping the design and fabric to a glass pane in a sunny window achieves the same effect.

TRACING PAPER METHOD

For dark or heavy fabrics, use dressmaker's tracing paper to transfer the design.

Place the fabric face up on a hard surface. Cover it with dressmaker's tracing paper in a color close to the fabric color but different enough to be visible; top both with a copy of the design. Tape the layers, if desired, to prevent shifting. Use a pencil, empty pen, ball point stylus (used for dry embossing) or similar tool to trace the design lines, checking frequently to ensure the design is transferring properly to the fabric.

COMPUTER PRINTING METHOD

If the project fabric is smaller than $8\frac{1}{2}$" × 11" (21.6cm × 27.9cm), a computer and printer can be used to transfer the design to fabric.

Press freezer paper to the fabric wrong side as directed above, then trim to exactly $8\frac{1}{2}$" × 11" (21.6cm × 27.9 cm). Lay the paper-backed fabric in the printer's paper tray, orienting it so the design will print on the fabric side. Lower the print quality to draft so less ink will be deposited on the fabric, then print.

If desired, open the graphics file in software that allows color changes and print the design in grey, light blue or a color that will match the embroidery thread. Remove the freezer paper and stitch the design.

Note: *Designs transferred this way are not colorfast, nor are the lines guaranteed to fade or wash away. Use computer printing only for guidelines that will be covered by embroidery.*

Computer-Printed Design on Fabric
Design #ANI029 was transferred in red by printing to freezer paper-backed fabric.

Creating a Mirror Image

Some home printers include options for reversing graphics. Consult your printer's manual for information. *Design: #ANI028.*

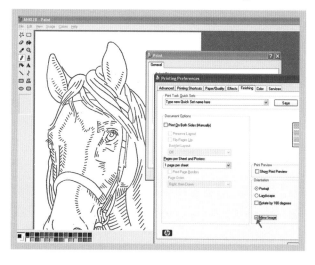

IRON-ON METHOD

The designs in this book were originally published as iron-on transfers; you can use print-outs from the CD-ROM to make iron-on transfers at home.

Begin by creating a mirror image of the embroidery design, reversing the motif with a graphics program or photocopier. Some home printers also include an option to reverse graphics as they print. If the design is printed on vellum or thin paper and can be seen from the back, it may be possible to trace the design lines on the paper's wrong side to create the mirror image.

Some photocopied designs can be transferred directly to fabric by laying the photocopy face down on the fabric right side and pressing with a warm to hot iron, which transfers the toner to the fabric. Test first on a scrap, as the results vary. This technique will not work with copies made with an ink jet printer.

Special pencils and pens can be used to make iron-on transfers. Draw over the lines of the printed design as directed by the pen or pencil manufacturer. It is important to read and follow the directions carefully, as the sublimation inks used in transfer pens are permanent and mistakes cannot be removed from the fabric.

The pens are available in several colors including white for transferring designs to dark fabrics, although the white ink typically creates a wider line than other colors. Consider using an ink that matches your thread color to minimize the visibility of the transferred lines.

One inked transfer can be used several times, depending on the amount of ink on the transfer and the fiber content of the fabric. Transferred lines are typically brighter and more durable on synthetic fabrics than on pure cotton.

TAKE PRECAUTIONS

With any transfer method, it is important to protect the iron and pressing surface. Cover the ironing board with paper towels or a non-stick pressing sheet. Lay blank paper, a press cloth or another non-stick sheet over the transfer paper to protect the iron from bleeding ink.

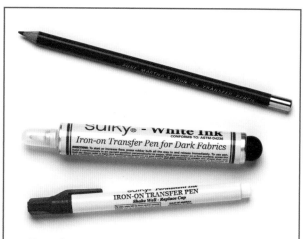

Transfer Pencil and Pens
Pencil by Aunt Martha's, pens by Sulky of America.

Transfer Tips

❀ Less-expensive papers often produce the best transfers.

❀ Transfer pen tips can become blunted over time, so keep a pen just for fine lines. Switch to an older pen when fine lines are less important.

stitches for hand-embroidered redwork

The simplicity of redwork extends to its small palette of stitches. Each is simple to work but contributes a unique texture and form to the overall embroidery.

The designs in this book, when worked at their original sizes, are ideally proportioned for two or three strands of six-strand embroidery floss. Pull an 18" (45.7cm) length of floss from the skein and separate it into individual strands. Recombine the number of strands desired for the embroidery and thread them into an embroidery or chenille needle.

Begin stitching by securing the thread on the fabric wrong side. The knot may be positioned close to the stitches and left in place after embroidering, or a waste knot can be used. With a waste knot, the knot lies on the fabric right side about 3" (7.6cm) from the first stitches. When embroidery is complete, cut away the knot, thread the tail into the needle, and weave the thread tail through several stitches on the wrong side of the work to secure it.

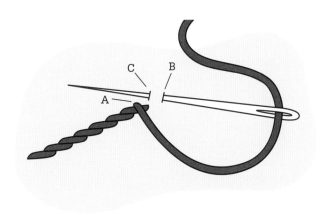

Outline or Stem Stitch

OUTLINE OR STEM STITCH

Outline or stem stitch is the primary stitch used in redwork for outlining designs. Sometimes a distinction is made between the two names, based on the relative positions of the needle and thread, but the names are used interchangeably here.

Working from left to right, bring the needle to the right side of the fabric at A. Stitch back into the fabric at B, $\frac{1}{8}$" (3mm) to $\frac{1}{4}$" (6mm) away from A. Bring the needle to the right side again at C, which lies halfway between A and B. This becomes point A for the next stitch.

Continue along the design line, consistently bringing the needle to the right side above (or below) the line of stitches. The stitched result resembles twisted cord.

BACKSTITCH

Backstitch is similar to the outline stitch and is a fine alternative for redwork. The stitches share holes but do not overlap as in the outline stitch.

Working from right to left, bring the needle up at *A*. Insert the needle at *B* about ⅛" (3mm) behind or to the right of *A*, then bring the needle up at *C*; pull through, then insert the needle again at *A*, using the same needle hole. Continue along the design line, keeping the stitches a consistent length.

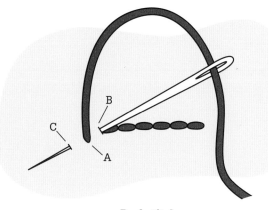

Backstitch

FRENCH KNOTS

French knots are worked by wrapping the thread around the needle and pulling the needle and thread through the wraps. In redwork, French knots are often used for eyes, flower centers and other decorative details.

To make, bring the thread to the right side at the desired location (*A*) and wrap it twice around the needle near the bottom of the thread where it emerges from the fabric. Insert the needle back into the fabric at *B*, just two or three threads away from *A*, gently pulling the thread enough to tighten the wraps on the needle. Hold the knot in place as you pull the needle and thread through to the other side of the fabric.

For larger French knots, wrap the thread three or four times around the needle or use more strands of floss.

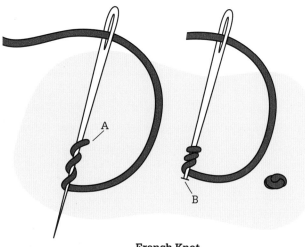

French Knot

SATIN STITCH

Satin stitch is used to fill certain areas of the fabric with solid color, so it is used sparingly in redwork. It is important to use a hoop while working satin stitches.

Bring the needle up through the fabric on one side of the area and take it back down through the fabric on the opposite side. Come up again to the side of the first stitch and continue until the space is filled, placing the stitches side by side but not overlapping. Taper the length of the stitches according to the dimensions of the shape you're filling. Keep the stitches taut, but do not pull the thread so tightly that the background fabric buckles under the stitches.

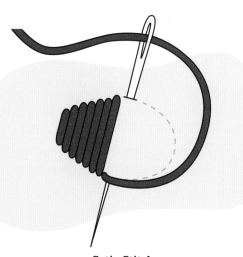

Satin Stitch

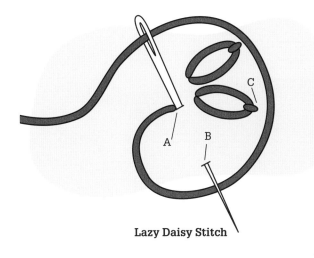

Lazy Daisy Stitch

LAZY DAISY STITCH

The lazy daisy stitch, in the shape of a flower petal, is made by creating a loop on the fabric surface, then securing the loop with a tiny stitch. To work, bring the needle up through the fabric at the bottom of the loop position (*A*). Take the needle back through the fabric at *A* and rock the needle so it emerges at *B*, but do not pull the thread yet. Make sure the thread is looped under the needle, then pull the thread through the fabric, leaving a little slack in the thread for a pleasing loop. Bring the needle back down at the tip of the loop (*C*), just on the other side of the thread, tacking the loop into place.

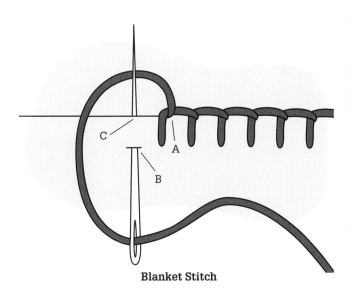

Blanket Stitch

BLANKET STITCH

Blanket stitch is often used as an edging, but it can also be worked as a decorative stitch for flower centers, petals and other areas of a motif. The horizontal and vertical arms of the stitch are usually the same length (between ⅛" [3mm] and ¼" [6mm]), although they can be varied for special effects. Position the horizontal line of the stitch on a design outline with the stitch arms pointing inward.

Bring the needle to the right side at *A*. Insert the needle into the fabric again at *B* and rock the needle to emerge at *C*, with the *A-B* thread under the needle. Pull the needle through to complete the stitch.

To end a line of blanket stitches, take the needle back into the fabric a few threads from the last *C* and over the final *A-B* thread. If the stitches enclose a circle or other shape, end by taking the last *A-B* thread under the first *A-B* thread, then take the needle to the wrong side of the fabric at the final point *B*.

redwork projects

Embroidery designs, no matter how wonderful, are only lines and shapes (or computer ones and zeros) until they are stitched into a project! This section presents a dozen project ideas to get you started, but feel free to expand the possibilities using your favorite materials and techniques.

Some projects have been designed with gift-giving in mind: the *Hemstitched Linen Towel* (page 76) and *Case for Travel Pillow* (page 48), for example. A few are quick and easy, requiring only one or a few designs, such as the *Basic Tote Bag* (page 44) and *Framed Sentiments* (page 94). Others, like the *Redwork Quilt* that showcases fifty-eight motifs (page 36), represent a significant investment of time and produce heirloom results.

There are also photographs of purchased blanks embellished with some of the book's designs. Redwork's simplicity and speedy stitching combined with premade blanks are truly a recipe for quick and easy crafting.

If you're hand-embroidering the motifs for these projects, please note that you may have to resize the motifs first. See *Changing Design Size*, page 22, for more about resizing the designs from the CD-ROM.

REDWORK QUILT

Originally, redwork embroidery adorned dishtowels, laundry bags, pillowcases and other household linens, but not quilts. Perhaps it was the popularity of preprinted penny squares that led needleworkers to make quilts by piecing together the many simple squares they embroidered. Whether you embroider by hand or machine, this quilt is a marvelous showcase for dozens of redwork motifs. Pad it with batting, as described below, or omit the batting layer for a lightweight summer quilt like those popular with nineteenth century embroiderers.

what you'll need

See **Fabric Note** *on page 38.*

2¾ yds. (2.5m) darkest red fabric (#1)

3 yds. (2.7m) medium dark red fabric (#2)

2⅜ yds. (2.1m) medium red fabric (#3)

½ yd. (45.7cm) light red fabric (#4)

2 yd. (1.8m) off-white fabric

2½ yds. (2.3m) backing fabric, 118" (3m) wide

Embroidery*, sewing and bobbin threads

Lightweight tear-away stabilizer for embroidery

Quilt batting

Fabrics for our quilt were provided by Paintbrush Studio Collections, a division of Fabri-Quilt, Inc.

Warm & White batting for our quilt was furnished by The Warm Company.

Quilted by Lynn Mullins of Aunt Lynn's Long Arm Quilting.

*Embroidered with Coats & Clark's Dual Duty XP All Purpose thread for a traditional matte finish.

DESIGNS *on* CD-ROM

**54 designs of choice
for the 4" × 4"
(100mm x 100mm) hoop**

**2 vertical designs of choice
for the 5" × 7"
(130mm × 180mm) hoop**

**2 horizontal designs of choice
for the 5" × 7"
(130mm × 180mm) hoop**

(see Key to Designs on CD-ROM,
pages 102–119)

Finished size: 79" × 95" (2m × 2.4m)

instructions

Seam allowance is ¼" (6mm),
and is included in all cutting dimensions.

CUTTING THE FABRIC

NOTE: *For easier hooping, the off-white blocks (I, J1, J2) can be cut after embroidery. Extra fabric is included in the yardage requirement.*

{
FABRIC NOTE
Fabric requirements are based on 100% cotton fabrics with at least 42" (1.1m) usable width. Use value variations to create contrast in this two-color quilt by choosing fabric prints that range from dark (primarily red with some lighter areas) to light (primarily off-white with some red areas).

CUTTING CHART FOR *Redwork Quilt*

* Cut these border pieces first on the lengthwise grain.
Use the remaining fabric to cut squares, sashing strips and binding strips.

The border pieces are cut with extra length.
See the instructions for information on measuring the quilt and trimming the borders to fit.

FABRIC	LOCATION	SIZE	QUANTITY	PATCH NAME
Red #1	Inner border*	2" × 75" (5.1cm × 191cm)	4	--
	Sashing strips	2" × 5½" (5.1cm × 14cm)	216	A
	Sashing strips	2" × 6½" (5.1cm × 16.5cm)	8	B
	Sashing strips	2" × 8½" (5.1cm × 21.6cm)	8	C
Red #2	Outer border*	7½" × 84" (19cm × 213cm)	4	--
	Center square	2½" × 2½" (6.4cm × 6.4cm)	1	D
	Binding	2" (5.1cm) × fabric width	10	--
Red #3	Middle border*	3½" × 78" (8.9cm × 198cm)	4	--
	Internal border	2½" × 20½" (6.4cm × 52cm)	2	E
	Internal border	2½" × 24½" (6.4cm × 62.2cm)	2	F
	Sashing squares	2" × 2" (5.1cm × 5.1cm)	116	G
Red #4	Sashing squares	2" × 2" (5.1cm × 5.1cm)	116	H
Off-white	Block centers	5½" × 5½" (14cm × 14cm)	54	I
	Block centers	6½" × 8½" (16.5cm × 21.6cm)	2	J1 (horizontal)
	Block centers	8½" × 68½" (21.6cm × 16.5cm)	2	J2 (vertical)

EMBROIDERING THE DESIGNS

1 Embroider the 54 smaller redwork designs on off-white fabric, hooping the fabric and tear-away stabilizer together. Remove the stabilizer after embroidery, press carefully and trim each block to 5½" (14cm) square (*I* in the cutting chart on page 38).

2 Embroider the four larger redwork designs as in Step 1. Be sure to create two blocks 6½" (16.5cm) high (*J1* in the cutting chart on page 38) and two blocks 8½" (21.6cm) high (*J2* in the cutting chart); that is, two with horizontal designs and two with vertical. Trim the blocks to 6½" × 8½" (16.5cm × 21.6cm).

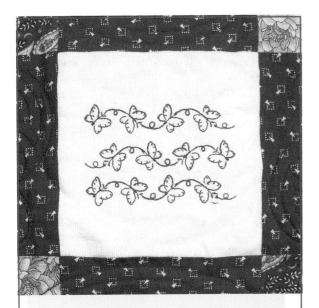

Smallest Designs

To use the smallest motifs from the CD-ROM, embroider several designs or multiple copies of a single design to better fill the block.

The Look of Hand Embroidery

For richer color and heavier texture reminiscent of hand embroidery, use the same thread in both needle and bobbin.

PIECING THE EMBROIDERED BLOCKS

1 Stitch *A* rectangles to the left and right sides of each embroidered *I* square.

2 Sew a *G* square to one end of each unattached *A* rectangle. Sew *H* squares to the other ends of the same *A* rectangles.

3 Sew these *G-A-H* units to the top and bottom of the embroidered *A-I-A* units. Position the *G* squares at the top left and bottom right corners of each pieced block.

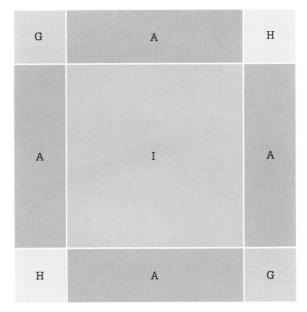

Block Piecing Diagram for Embroidered Squares

4 Sew B rectangles to the left and right sides of the two horizontal blocks (J1 in the diagram below). Sew C rectangles to the left and right sides of the two vertical blocks (J2 in the diagram below).

5 Stitch a G square to one end of each unattached B and C rectangle. Stitch H squares to the other ends.

6 Sew the G-B-H units to the top and bottom of the two vertical blocks (J2). Sew the G-C-H units to the top and bottom of the two horizontal blocks (J1). Be sure the G squares are at the top left and bottom right corners of each pieced block.

7 Arrange the four units from Step 6 as shown in the quilt layout below. Place the D patch in the center of the group.

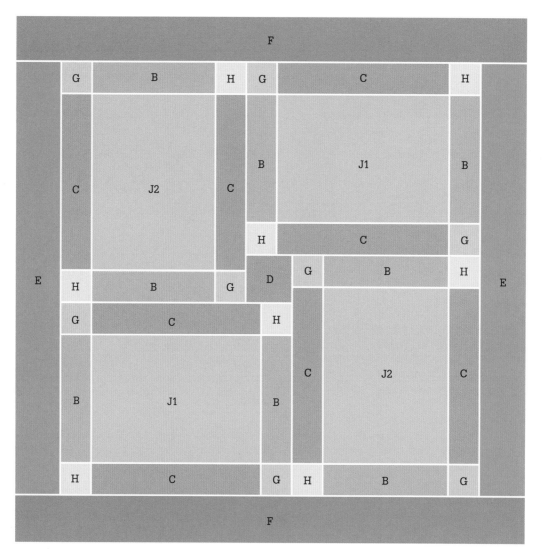

Piecing Diagram for Quilt Center
Piecing the J1 and J2 blocks.

ASSEMBLE THE CENTRAL UNIT

1 Sew *D* to the embroidered and pieced block at the top left, matching the lower raw edges. Begin stitching ¾" (1.9cm) from the raw edge of *D*, and sew all the way to the lower raw edges.

2 Stitch the bottom left block to the first block and the *D* patch.

3 Sew the two remaining embroidered and pieced blocks to those already sewn, proceeding counterclockwise around the *D* patch.

4 Stitch the last (upper right) block to the first (upper left), sewing from the raw edge to the beginning of the partial seam from Step 1, to complete the pieced central area.

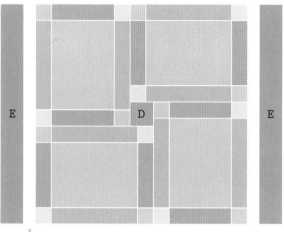

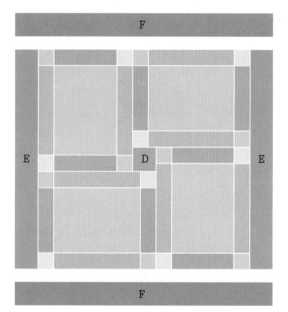

5 Sew the *E* strips to the sides of the central piecing.

6 Stitch the *F* strips to the top and bottom of the central unit to complete.

CONSTRUCTING THE REST OF THE QUILT

1 Decide where each of the other motifs will be placed in the quilt. Arrange the blocks into nine rows of seven blocks, replacing the nine blocks at the center with the unit pieced in Step 7 (see the color layout diagram on page 43 and the black-and-white line diagram on page 123).

2 Stitch the top three rows together.

3 Assemble the bottom three rows of pieced blocks.

4 Make six short rows (two blocks each) to lie beside the central unit, and assemble them into two groups as shown. Sew these units to the central pieced square.

A Great Quilt Deserves a Great Label
Combine embroidery and ink jet-printable fabric for a label as unique as the quilt. *Design: #MSC041. Fonts: Bernhard Fashion BT, Enviro.*

Layout for *Redwork Quilt*
A black-and-white line diagram of this layout is available on page 123.

5 Sew the top and bottom rows to the central portion of the quilt.

6 Measure the quilt top from top to bottom through the middle. Cut two inner border strips to this measurement and stitch one to each side of the pieced quilt top.

7 Measure the quilt top and borders from side to side through the middle. Cut the two remaining inner border strips to this measurement and stitch to the top and bottom of the pieced quilt top.

8 Repeat Steps 6–7 to attach the middle border pieces to the quilt, then repeat again to add the outer border.

9 Layer the quilt top, batting and backing. Baste. Quilt as desired through all three layers. Trim the backing and batting to match the quilt top.

10 Join the binding strips into one continuous length. Press in half, lengthwise, wrong sides together. Bind the quilt top, mitering the corners.

BASIC TOTE BAG

A basic tote provides a home for craft projects, acts as a gift bag or carries purchases. Customize a bag with any embroidery design from our big collection: a cowboy book bag, vegetable shopping bags, or a heart-embellished Valentine's Day bag.

With so many uses for a basic tote bag, why make just one?

what you'll need

See **Fabric Note** *on page 46.*

1 yd. (0.9m) sturdy fabric, 45" (1.1m) wide
(Suggestions: denim, poplin, bottom weight sportswear fabrics)

1¼ yd. (1.1m) webbing, 1" (2.5cm) wide (handles)

Embroidery, bobbin and sewing threads

Iron-on tear-away stabilizer

Removable marking tool

DESIGN *on* CD-ROM

#MSC041

(see Key to Designs on CD-ROM, *pages 102–119)*

instructions

Seam allowance is ¼" (6mm).

NOTE: *A serger makes quick work of totes like this one. Serge the tote side and boxing seams to construct and finish in one step. If a serger is unavailable, stitch the seams with a conventional sewing machine and use an overcasting or zigzag stitch to finish the raw edges.*

Use the serger to finish the top raw edge rather than pressing ¼" (6mm) to the wrong side, and the hems will be less bulky.

FABRIC NOTE
For greatest strength and minimal stretch, cut the tote on the lengthwise grain; one yard (0.9m) of fabric makes two totes. If you prefer, purchase just ½ yard (45.7m) and cut the tote on the crosswise grain.

1 Cut a 15½" × 33" (39.4cm × 83.8cm) rectangle for the tote. Following the diagram, remove a rectangular area from each side edge.

2 Stabilize one end of the tote and mark an embroidery location 6" (15.2cm) from the upper edge and centered from side to side.

3 Embroider a redwork motif centered at the marked location. When stitching is complete, remove the stabilizer and press the work from the wrong side.

4 Fold the tote in half, right sides together, and sew or serge the tote side seams (see the note at the top of the left column about serging).

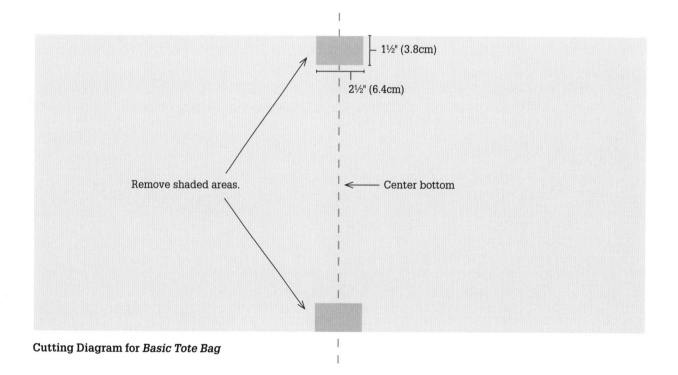

1½" (3.8cm)

2½" (6.4cm)

Remove shaded areas.

Center bottom

Cutting Diagram for *Basic Tote Bag*

Side Seam Aligned with the Center Bottom
Match the cutout edges and pin for the boxing seams.

5 Fold the tote so the side seam aligns with the center bottom, matching the edges of the rectangular cutout. Sew or serge the raw edges. Repeat to box the other side.

6 Press ¼" (6mm) to the wrong side along the tote top edge, then turn under an additional 1" (2.5cm) and press. Stitch the hem in place.

7 Cut the webbing into two 22" (55.9cm) lengths. Zigzag across the cut ends to prevent fraying.

8 Mark locations for the handles on the tote 4" (10cm) from each side seam. Position the handles inside the tote's upper edge with the webbing raw edge at the lower hem fold and the webbing outer edge at the marked location. Be sure the webbing is not twisted.

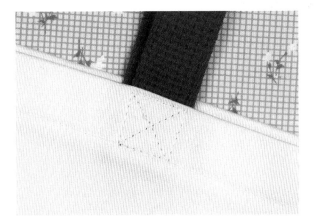

9 Stitch each handle end to the tote with an *X* inside a square, retracing stitches as required.

more ideas:

❀

Add a pocket of solid or tone-on-tone fabric to emphasize embroidery on a print fabric tote (upper left).

❀

Recycle promotional totes (lower left) by embroidering on plain fabric and fusing or stitching the embroidered panel over the printed logo. Cover the logo with iron-on interfacing to minimize show-through.

CASE FOR TRAVEL PILLOW

Take along a touch of home when you pack this attractive and functional travel pillow. With a hidden pocket to keep the pillow form in place, this little softie is perfect for travel by train, plane or automobile. It's small enough to stuff into a suitcase or tote, but big enough to add comfort when the journey's long. Use it at home, too; it's too pretty to hide away between trips!

what you'll need

¾ yd. (68.6cm) cotton sateen,
45" (1.1m) wide

Embroidery, bobbin and sewing threads

Iron-on tear-away stabilizer

12" × 16" (30.5cm × 40.6cm) travel pillow form

Water-soluble marking pen

Wing needle for hemstitching (optional)

DESIGN *on* CD-ROM

#MSC038

(see Key to Designs on CD-ROM,
pages 102–119)

instructions

Seam allowance is ½" (1.3cm).

CUTTING THE FABRIC

Cut a 13" × 20" (33cm × 50.8cm) rectangle for the pillowcase front and a 13" × 24" (33cm × 61cm) rectangle for the pillowcase back.

EMBROIDERING THE PILLOWCASE

1. Fold the pillowcase front in half lengthwise and crease lightly; unfold. Measure and mark across the crease 8" (20.3cm) from one short end. This marks the center point for the embroidery.

2. Cut iron-on tear-away stabilizer to fit the machine's 5" × 7" (130mm × 180mm) hoop and iron it to the fabric wrong side, centered on the cross marks.

3. Hoop the fabric and stitch the embroidery design, centered on the marked location.

4. Remove the placement marks and excess stabilizer. Place the embroidered fabric face down on a thick towel and press from the wrong side.

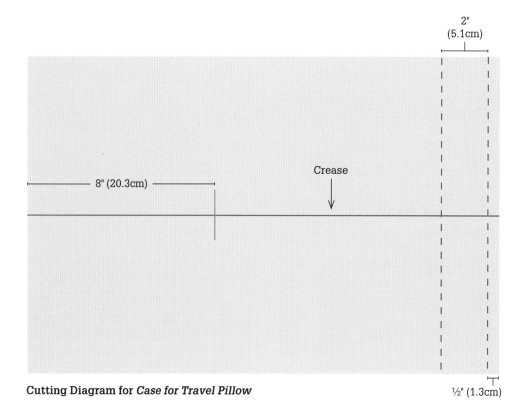

2"
(5.1cm)

8" (20.3cm)

Crease

½" (1.3cm)

Cutting Diagram for *Case for Travel Pillow*

White on Red
Stitch with white thread on a red or other solid-color pillowcase for a stunning effect. *Design:* #MSC044.

more ideas:

❀

*Stitch the pillowcase from muslin,
weaver's cloth or flannel.*

❀

*Use tiny French seams to finish a batiste pillowcase
for a delicate heirloom appearance.*

❀

*If the fabric has no obvious right and wrong sides,
turn the hem to the right side and finish with
contrasting piping rather than hemstitching.*

❀

*Stitch the redwork with glow-in-the-dark
thread for a fun bedtime surprise.*

❀

Embroider redwork on full-size pillowcases, too.

CONSTRUCTING THE PILLOWCASE

1 Press under ½" (1.3cm), then 2" (5.1cm) on the end of the pillowcase front that is farthest from the embroidery. Edge-stitch the hem, or insert a wing needle and use an entredeux or pinstitch to secure the hem.

2 Turn under ¼" (6mm) twice on one short end of the pillowcase back and edge-stitch.

3 Fold 6" (15.2cm) of the hemmed edge to the wrong side and press to form the pocket.

4 Lay the pillowcase front on the pillowcase back, right sides together, matching the hemmed ends. Stitch the sides and the un-finished end. Use a serger or set the sewing machine for an overcasting stitch to finish the seam allowances.

5 Turn the pillowcase right side out so the pocket lies between the front and back. Insert the pillow form, tucking it inside the pocket.

CIRCUS WALL QUILT

This little quilt is perfect for hanging on a wall, but it's also a handy size for a toddler to take along on trips. By piecing the quilt top before the designs are embroidered, a space large enough for the bigger clown motif is created at the quilt center. The quilt could feature the nursery rhyme designs from the CD-ROM instead, or stitch five floral motifs with different fabrics and color palette for a sophisticated alternative appropriate for any room.

what you'll need

See **Fabric Note** *on page 54.*

½ yd. (45.7cm) tone-on-tone beige fabric [#1]

½ yd. (45.7cm) darkest red fabric [#2]

⅛ yd. (11.4cm) medium red fabric [#3]

⅛ yd. (11.4cm) lightest red fabric [#4]

¾ yd. (68.6cm) backing fabric

Embroidery, sewing and bobbin threads

Iron-on tear-away stabilizer

Quilt batting

Removable marking tool

Warm & Safe batting for our quilt was furnished by The Warm Company.

DESIGNS *on* CD-ROM

#JUV072

#JUV073

#JUV074

#JUV075

#JUV076

(see Key to Designs on CD-ROM, *pages 102–119)*

instructions

Seam allowance is ¼" (6mm) and is included in all cutting dimensions.

CUTTING THE FABRIC

NOTE: *To accommodate the larger clown motif, this quilt top must be pieced before embroidering. Cut all pieces as directed.*

CUTTING CHART FOR *Circus Wall Quilt*

* If desired, purchase ¼ yard (22.9cm) of a striped fabric and cut the binding on the bias from the striped fabric instead.

FABRIC	LOCATION	SIZE	QUANTITY	PATCH NAME
#1	Piecing	4½" × 1½" (11.4cm × 3.8cm)	16	A
	Embroidery backgrounds	6½" × 6½" (16.5cm × 16.5cm)	5	--
#2	Border	3" × 23½" (7.6cm × 59.7cm)	2	--
	Border	3" × 18½" (7.6cm × 47cm)	2	--
	Piecing	1½" × 1½" (3.8cm × 3.8cm)	16	B
	Binding*	2" (5.1cm) × fabric width	3	--
#3	Piecing	4½" × 1½" (11.4cm × 3.8cm)	8	C
	Piecing	2½" × 1½" (6.4cm × 3.8cm)	8	D
#4	Piecing	2½" × 2½" (6.4cm × 6.4cm)	4	E

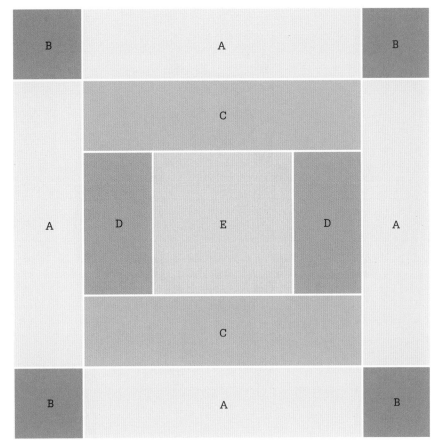

Block Piecing Diagram for *Circus Wall Quilt*

PIECING THE FOUR PATCHWORK BLOCKS

1. Sew *D* patches to two opposite sides of each *E* patch. Press the seams toward the *D* patches.

2. Stitch a *C* patch to each *D-E* unit, perpendicular to the existing seams, and press the seam allowance toward the *C*. Repeat to attach another *C* patch to the opposite side of the *D-E* unit.

3. Sew *A* patches to opposite sides of each pieced unit, parallel to the *D* patches. Press the seam allowances toward the *A* patches.

4. Stitch a *B* patch to each end of the unattached *A* patches. Press the seams toward the *A* patches.

5. Complete the blocks by sewing *A-B* units to the top and bottom of the central unit, perpendicular to the *A*s already sewn. Press the seam allowances toward the *A-B* units.

Layout Diagram for *Circus Wall Quilt*
A black-and-white line diagram of this layout is available on page 122.

CONSTRUCTING THE QUILT

1 Arrange the pieced blocks and the 6½" (16.5cm) squares as shown in the color layout diagram above and the black-and-white line diagram on page 122. Stitch the blocks and background squares into rows, then assemble the rows to make the quilt top.

2 Sew a 3" × 18½" (7.6cm x 47cm) border strip to each side of the quilt top. Press the seams toward the borders.

3 Stitch the remaining border strips to the top and bottom of the assembled quilt. Press the seam allowances toward the borders.

EMBROIDERING THE QUILT

1 Back the center square and surrounding portions of the pieced blocks with iron-on tear-away stabilizer large enough to fill the machine's 5" × 7" (130mm × 180mm) or larger hoop. Mark the block's center by drawing horizontal and vertical lines across the block with tailor's chalk or a removable marker.

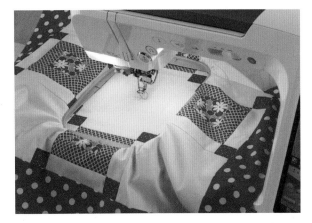

2 Hoop the quilt top and stitch the clown design, allowing the design lines to flow into the pieced blocks that surround the center square. **NOTE:** *The iron-on stabilizer will secure the seam allowances while the quilt top is hooped. Loosen the hoop's thumb screw to accommodate the thickness of the seam allowances.*

3 Cut a piece of iron-on tear-away stabilizer big enough for the hoop and press it onto the quilt wrong side with one plain corner block centered. Mark the block's center as described in Step 1. Hoop the quilt top with the stabilized block centered and embroider the first motif. After embroidering, remove the excess stabilizer.

4 Repeat Step 3 to embroider designs in the other three corner blocks.

5 When all embroidery is complete, remove any remaining stabilizer. Place the quilt top wrong side up on a folded towel or padded pressing surface and press the embroidered quilt top.

FINISHING THE QUILT

1 Layer the quilt top, batting and backing. Baste. Quilt as desired through all three layers. Trim the backing and batting to match the quilt top.

2 Join the binding strips into one continuous length. Press in half, lengthwise, wrong sides together. Bind the quilt top, mitering the corners.

more ideas:

✿

Add more squares to make a larger quilt,
or extend the quilt by adding an additional border.

✿

Sew a backing onto the pieced top
and insert a 24" (61cm) pillow form to make a floor pillow.

FOLDABLE SHOPPING TOTE

Folded, it's no bigger than a checkbook clutch, but this reusable shopping tote has plenty of room for purchases. It's small enough to fit inside a purse while folded, making it easy to have on hand for spur-of-the-moment purchases. Why not stitch several and keep a ready supply in the car?

what you'll need

1 yd. (0.9m) lightweight sturdy fabric, 45" (1.1m) wide *(Suggestions: poplin, ripstop cotton, lightweight denim)*

Embroidery, bobbin and sewing threads

Iron-on tear-away stabilizer

1½ yds. (1.4m) double-fold bias tape

1" (2.5cm) of hook and loop fastener, ¾" (1.9cm) wide

Removable marking tool

Built-in lettering: Brother's Quattro

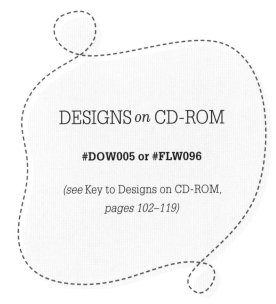

DESIGNS *on* CD-ROM

#DOW005 or #FLW096

(see Key to Designs on CD-ROM, *pages 102–119)*

Finished size: 16¼" × 15½" (41.3cm × 39.4cm) unfolded

instructions

Seam allowance is ¼" (6mm).

CUTTING THE FABRIC

1   Cut two 17½" × 16" (44.4cm × 40.6cm) pieces for the tote body and two 16" × 2½" (40.6cm × 6.3cm) strips for the handles.

2   Cut one rectangle 11½" × 7¾" (29.2cm × 19.7cm) for the pocket. Photocopy the template on this page, enlarging to 200%. Cut it out and use it to shape one short end of the pocket rectangle.

EMBROIDERING THE BAG

1   Back the pocket fabric with iron-on tear-away stabilizer large enough to fill the 5" × 7" (130mm × 180mm) hoop. Mark the design placement on the pocket piece 6" (15.2cm) from the straight end and centered side to side, with the top of the design toward the straight pocket end.

2   Hoop the stabilized fabric and embroider the design. When stitching is complete, remove the excess stabilizer and press the embroidery carefully from the wrong side.

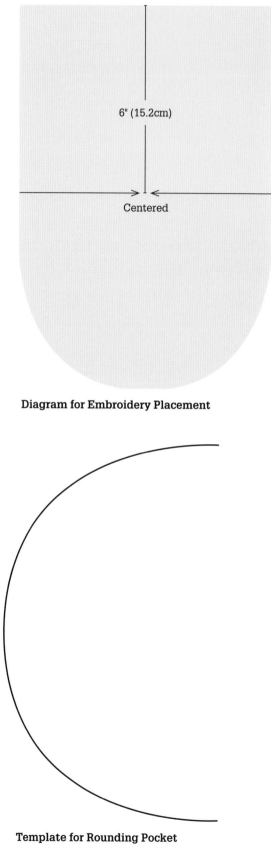

6" (15.2cm)

Centered

Diagram for Embroidery Placement

Template for Rounding Pocket
To use, enlarge to 200%.

CONSTRUCTING THE BAG

1 Bind the straight pocket edge with double-fold bias tape.

2 Press under ¼" (6mm) at one end of the remaining bias tape and bind the sides and curved end of the pocket piece. Stop just short of the final corner and cut the bias ¼" (6mm) beyond the pocket end. Turn under the ¼" (6mm) allowance and finish stitching the binding in place.

3 Sew the loop portion of the hook and loop fastener (A in photo) to the pocket right side, 2" (5.1cm) below the straight end and centered side to side. Sew the hook portion (B in photo) to the pocket wrong side along the curved edge and centered between the sides.

4 To make the handles, fold each strip in half lengthwise, right sides together, and stitch the long edges. Turn the handles right side out and press with the seam at one edge. Edge-stitch both long edges of each handle.

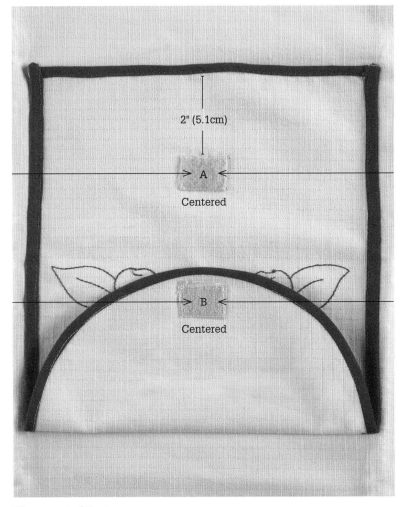

2" (5.1cm)

> A <
Centered

> B <
Centered

Placement of Fasteners
See Step 3, *Constructing the Bag*, and position the hook and loop fastener pieces as shown above.

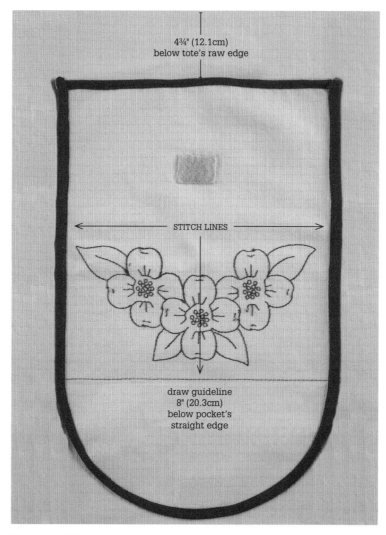

4¾" (12.1cm)
below tote's raw edge

STITCH LINES

draw guideline
8" (20.3cm)
below pocket's
straight edge

Steps 5 and 6
See Steps 5 and 6; position and stitch the pocket to the tote body as shown.

5 Pin the pocket to one tote rectangle, centered from side to side and with the straight pocket edge 4¾" (12.1cm) below the tote raw edge.

6 Draw a removable guideline 8" (20.3cm) below the pocket's straight end. Stitch the pocket to the tote along the sides and the guideline. Stitch over the previous seam attaching the binding to the pocket and reinforce the seam with backstitching at each end.

7 Place the tote pieces right sides together and stitch the side and bottom seams. Use a serger or an overcasting stitch on a regular

sewing machine to reinforce the seams and prevent raveling.

8 Pin the handles to the tote 4¼" (10.8cm) from the side seams, right sides together and raw edges matched. Baste ⅛" (3mm) from the raw edge.

9 Turn under ¼" (6mm) on the tote and handle raw edges and press. Turn under and press an additional ¾" (19.1mm). Stitch the hem near its bottom fold and edge-stitch along the top fold, stitching through the handles as well.

folding the bag

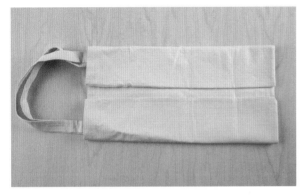

1 Fold the sides to the back along the pocket sides.

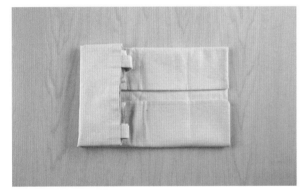

2 Fold the handles down, and fold the tote along the pocket straight edge.

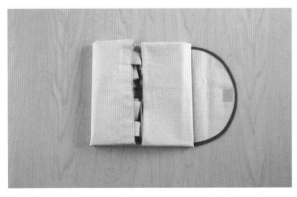

3 Fold the tote bottom upward along the line of stitching across the pocket.

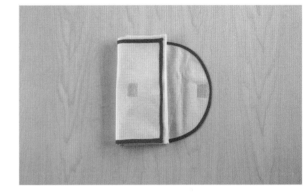

4 Fold the pocket straight edge over the other pocket folds.

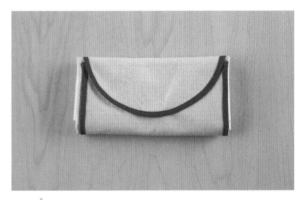

5 Bring the curved pocket end up, matching the hook and loop fasteners, and close the clutch.

The Folded Tote
Front and back views of the totes folded up for easy carrying.

SCALLOPED APRON

For a fun retro silhouette, showcase happy tea set motifs on a gored and scalloped apron. Flaring gores and gathers at the waistline give this apron a flirty twirl. The colored fabric gores framing the embroidered muslin can be any color you choose, or select a fun kitchen print and redwork designs that carry out the fabric theme.

what you'll need

See **Fabric Note** *on page 66.*

1¼ yds. (1.1m) muslin or light color cotton

1 yd. (0.9m) red print

Embroidery, bobbin and sewing threads

Iron-on tear-away or wash-away stabilizer

Paper for pattern
(use wrapping paper or freezer paper, or tape smaller pieces of paper together to create the size needed)

Water-soluble marking pen

Pencil

DESIGNS *on* CD-ROM

#HOM087,
#HOM088
#HOM089

(see Key to Designs on CD-ROM, *pages 102–119)*

instructions

Seam allowance is ¼" (6mm).

PREPARING THE PATTERN

1 Cut an 8½" × 20" (21.6cm x 50.8cm) rectangle of pattern paper. Fold the pattern paper in half lengthwise to create a 4¼" × 20" (10.8cm x 50.8cm) rectangle.

2 Measure 2¼" (5.7cm) from the open edges at the top and make a small mark. Measure ¼" (6mm) from the open edges at the bottom and make a second mark.

3 Use a long straightedge to connect the two marks. Cut along the line and discard the scraps; unfold the pattern and mark it *GORE*. Draw a grainline along the center fold.

4 Enlarge the scallop template on page 67 to 200%. Cut out and label this piece *TEMPLATE*.

{ **FABRIC NOTE**
All fabrics are woven cotton with at least 42" (1.1m) usable width unless noted.

CUTTING THE FABRIC

1 From the muslin, cut ten gores. **NOTE:** *Vary the direction of the gores, alternating the large and small pattern ends, for the most economical fabric usage.*

2 From the red print, cut:
- Four gores
- Two strips 6½" (16.5cm) wide across the fabric width for the ties
- One rectangle 3½" × 18½" (8.9cm × 47cm) for the waistband

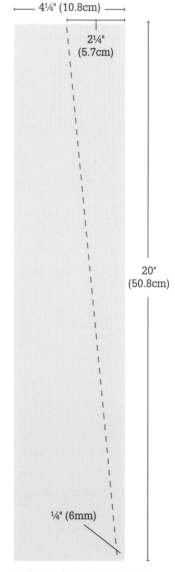

├── 4¼" (10.8cm) ──┤

2¼" (5.7cm)

20" (50.8cm)

¼" (6mm)

Making the Gore Pattern

EMBROIDERING THE APRON

1 Choose the tea cup, sugar bowl and creamer designs (#HOM087, #HOM088 and #HOM089) or any other 4" × 4" (100mm x 100mm) motifs.

2 On three muslin gores, mark an embroidery location 3¾" (9.5cm) above the bottom edge and centered from side to side.

3 Following the manufacturer's instructions for iron temperature, press stabilizer onto the wrong side of each gore. Cut the stabilizer large enough to fill the embroidery hoop and center it on the marked embroidery location, allowing it to extend beyond the gore edges if necessary.

4 Hoop and embroider one motif on each marked gore. Remove the excess stabilizer and press the embroidered panels face down on a padded surface.

CONSTRUCTING THE APRON

1 Alternating red print and embroidered muslin gores, sew seven gores together. Press the seams to the right.

2 Sew the remaining seven muslin gores together to make the lining. Press the seam allowances to the right.

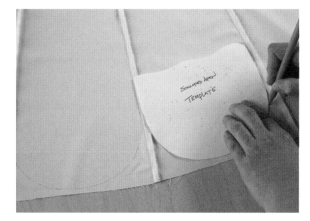

3 Lay the assembled lining on the work surface, wrong side up.

Position the template on the first gore, matching the side seam lines, with the template lower edge ¼" (6mm) above the fabric edge. Trace the curved edge of the template onto the fabric.

Repeat to trace the curve on each of the seven lining sections. This creates the stitching line for the apron hem.

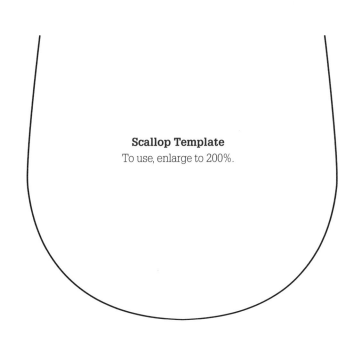

Scallop Template
To use, enlarge to 200%.

4 Pin the lining to the apron, right sides together, matching the lower edges and seams. Sew the apron and lining together, beginning at the upper (waistline) edge. Stitch directly on the curved lines, then pivot again and sew the side seam up to the waistline raw edge.

Extra Space Allowance

As you pivot between scallops, take one stitch across the seam between gores. This stitch provides a tiny amount of extra room for the seam allowances when the scallops are turned right side out.

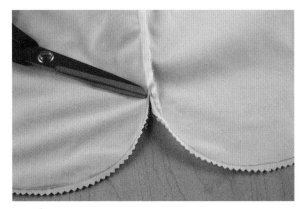

5 Notch the seam allowances along the curved edge and clip into the seam allowance at each gore-joining seam, taking care not to clip the hemline stitches.

One Step to Uniform Spacing

Use pinking shears to trim and notch curved seams in one step. This creates uniformly spaced notches for a smoother curve.

6 Turn the lining and apron right side out. Use a point turner or knitting needle to smooth the curves and create neat corners. Press.

7 Sew gathering stitches along the apron's upper edge, ¼" (6mm) and ⅛" (3mm) from the raw edge, stitching through both the apron and lining.

8 Press the waistband in half lengthwise, wrong sides together. Open the fold and press ¼" (6mm) to the wrong side along one long edge of the waistband.

9 Pin the apron to the waistband along the edge that is not pressed, right sides together, leaving ¼" (6mm) of the waistband free at each end. Draw up the gathering stitches to fit and distribute the gathers evenly. Stitch the waistband to the apron, press the seam toward the waistband and remove the gathering stitches.

10 Fold each tie in half lengthwise, right sides together. Stitch one short end, pivot, and stitch the long edge. Trim the corners and turn the ties right side out. Press.

more ideas:

❀

If you prefer, skip Step 3
under Constructing the Apron *and*
make an apron with a straight bottom edge.

❀

Add more gores and an elastic waistband
for a simple skirt.

❀

Embroider an apron blank for the quickest
of projects (see the photo at left).

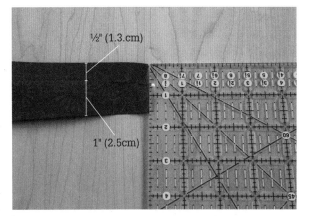

½" (1.3 cm)

1" (2.5cm)

11 Pleat the open end of each tie so it measures 1½" (3.8cm). Baste across the pleat to secure.

12 Pin one tie to each short end of the waistband, right sides together and raw edges matched, positioning the tie seam at the waistband seam. Fold the waistband in half, right sides together, covering the ties, and stitch the short ends.

13 Clip the corners and turn the waistband to the right side, pressing the ties away from the waistband. Match the waistband's pressed edge to the apron/waistband seam and stitch in place invisibly by hand.

Flower-of-the-Month Banner

This simple banner creates an easily changed display for monthly designs or any collection of similarly sized motifs. The secret it conceals makes changing designs seasonally, for special occasions or "just because" as easy as can be.

what you'll need

See Fabric Note *on page 72.*

3/8 yd. (34.3cm) main fabric

1/8 yd. (11.4cm) contrast fabric

3/8 yd. (34.3cm) flannel

Solid or tone-on-tone fabric for interchangeable embroidered panels

Embroidery, bobbin and sewing threads

Stabilizer for embroidery

Pencil or marking tool

DESIGNS *on* CD-ROM

#FOM008–#FOM019
or others as desired

(see Key to Designs on CD-ROM, *pages 102–119)*

Finished size: 10½" × 10½" (26.7cm × 26.7cm)

A Flowered Panel for Every Month

Designs #FOM008–#FOM019 on the CD-ROM provide monthly blossoms to embroider, complete with lettering.

See the design key on pages 102-119 for additional options for creating interchangeable embroidered panels.

instruction

Seam allowance is ¼" (6mm).

CUTTING THE FABRIC

1 From the main fabric, cut:

- One 10½" (26.7cm) square for backing

- Two 2" × 10½" (5.1cm × 26.7cm) rectangles for border

- Two 2" × 7½" (5.1cm × 19cm) rectangles for border

- Two 2" × 32" (5.1cm × 81.3cm) strips for binding

NOTE: *For best fabric usage, cut the 10½" (26.7cm) square first, then cut 2" (5.1cm) strips from the remaining fabric, cross-cutting as necessary to make the rectangles.*

2 From the contrast fabric, cut four 2½" × 7½" (6.3cm × 19cm) rectangles for the flanges.

3 From the flannel, cut one 10½" (26.7cm) square.

4 Cut the solid-color fabric(s) into 6½" (16.5cm) squares either before or after embroidery.

 FABRIC NOTE
All fabrics are woven cotton with at least 42" (1.1m) usable width unless noted.

EMBROIDERING THE INSERT

1. Embroider a single motif at the center of each 6½" (16.5cm) square, using appropriate stabilizer. If the squares are cut before embroidering, hoop adhesive stabilizer and attach the fabric to the stabilizer for embroidery. Because the back will be hidden, tear-away stabilizer can be used, but consider a water-soluble stabilizer if the embroidered square will be reused in another project (see *More Ideas* on page 75).

2. Remove the stabilizer and press the embroidered fabric from the wrong side. Pink or serge the fabric raw edges.

CONSTRUCTING THE BANNER

1. Lay the backing rectangle on a work surface wrong side up. Smooth the flannel, right side up, onto the backing, matching the raw edges.

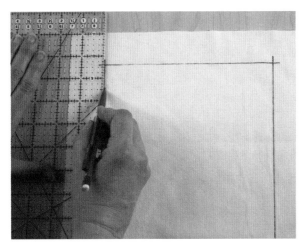

2. With a fabric marker, pencil or chalk, draw lines 1½" (3.8cm) from each edge of the flannel, creating a 7½" (19cm) square where the lines intersect at the center. (See the diagram on this page.) **NOTE:** *These lines will not be visible in the finished project.*

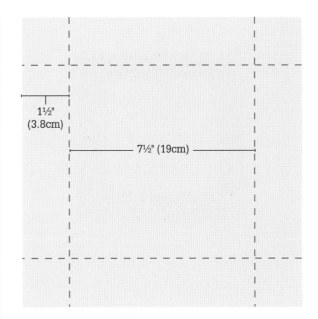

1½"
(3.8cm)

7½" (19cm)

Flange Placement Lines

3. Press the flanges in half lengthwise, wrong sides together. Position a flange right side up along the left edge of the drawn square, matching the flange raw edges to the marked lines, with the flange fold toward the project's center. Pin.

4. Position a second flange right side up along the right edge of the center square, matching raw edges, and pin.

73

5 Place the last two flanges right side up along the top and bottom of the 7½" (19cm) square, overlapping the flanges already in place, and pin. The flange folds will border a 5" (12.7cm) square of flannel left visible at the project center.

6 Lay one 2" × 7½" (5.1cm × 19cm) border rectangle face down along the left side of the 7½" (19cm) square. The border rectangle will cover the flanges, with raw edges matching along the 7½" (19cm) square. Stitch the border rectangle to the project through all layers, back-tacking at each end. Open the seam and press the border rectangle into place, covering the flannel outside the central square.

7 Position the second 2" × 7½" (5.1cm × 19cm) border rectangle face down along the right side of the flange square. Stitch through all layers, back-tacking at each end, then open the seam and press the border rectangle into place.

8 Stitch the 2" × 10½" (5.1cm × 26.7cm) border rectangles to the top and bottom of the flange square, back-tacking as before. Press into place.

9 Join the binding segments to create a continuous strip. Press in half lengthwise, wrong sides together. Bind the hanging, mitering the corners.

10 To use the hanging, lift the folded edges of the flanges slightly and slip an embroidered square into place. The flannel backing holds the square securely until it's time for a change, and the flanges cover the square's raw edges.

more ideas:

❀

*For a larger hanging, make more squares, eliminating the backing.
Sew the squares together, then add a single backing and bind as one unit.
(By turning the embroidered panels within the flanges, the completed
hanging can be hung horizontally or vertically, as shown in the photos.)*

❀

*Stitch one design a month, and at the end of the year
join all twelve motifs to create a larger wall hanging or quilt.*

❀

*If a wall hanging doesn't suit your décor, use the hanging
(without the backing) as the front of a throw pillow.
Add another border, if necessary, to create the correct size
for your pillow form.*

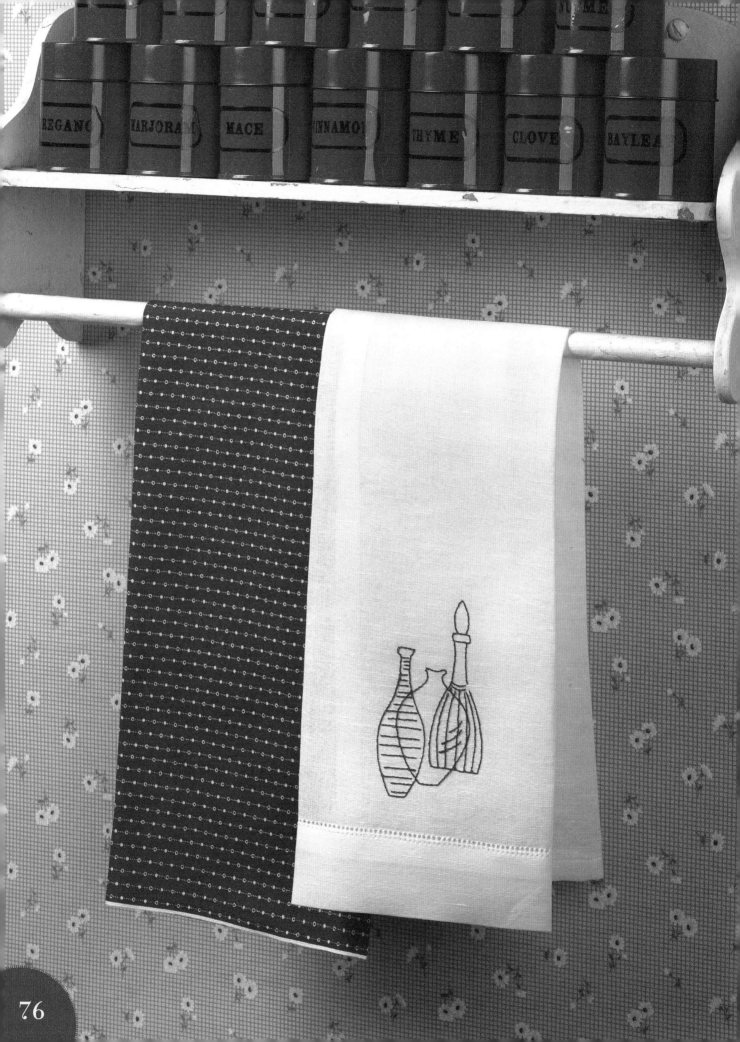

Hemstitched Linen Towel

Linen is a wonderful fiber to use and to embellish with embroidery. Whether in pristine white or casual colors, hand towels made from crisp linen are a luxurious decoration for a guest bathroom; and with linen's natural absorbency, they are highly functional, too. Make a stack of linen towels and decorate them with a variety of motifs and colors for gifts or personal use.

what you'll need

¾ yd. (68.6cm) medium-weight linen,
45" (1.1m) wide (enough fabric for 2 towels)

Embroidery, heirloom, and sewing threads*

Spray starch

Removable marking tool

Wing needle, size 100/16

*Use embroidery thread in both needle and bobbin
for a reversible appearance. Select an heirloom-weight
thread (60 or 80) for the wing needle work.

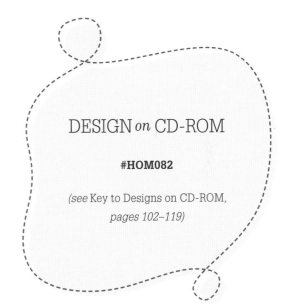

DESIGN *on* CD-ROM

#HOM082

(*see* Key to Designs on CD-ROM,
pages 102–119)

Finished size: 14" × 22" (35.6cm × 55.9cm)

instructions

PREPARING THE FABRIC

1 Pull a single linen thread from the fabric near the cut edge. If the thread breaks, cut along the gap left by the thread removal, pick up the thread at the break and continue pulling and cutting across the entire fabric width.

2 Measure along the fabric length and pull a second thread 25" (63.5cm) from the first. Pull and cut across the entire fabric width.

3 Pull and cut along a thread near one selvage to remove the selvage from the fabric. Measure 16" (40.6cm) from this edge and pull and cut along a thread, creating a 16" × 25" (40.6cm × 63.5cm) rectangle.

EMBROIDERING THE TOWEL

1 Spray the linen wrong side with starch and press. Be sure the linen is squared on the ironing board, with its warp and weft threads crossing at right angles. Repeat once or twice until the linen is stiffened.

Stabilizing the Linen

To ensure the starch provides enough stabilization for embroidery, test first on a fabric scrap. Use water-soluble stabilizer under the linen if necessary.

2 Fold the linen rectangle in half lengthwise, and finger press to crease. Measure 6" (15.2cm) from one 16" (40.6cm) end and mark across the centerline to indicate the embroidery location. **NOTE:** *To adjust the placement for different embroidery motifs, position the design so its lower edge is 4⅛" (10.5cm) from the linen edge.*

3 Thread both needle and bobbin with embroidery thread. Hoop the starched linen and embroider the design. Remove the markings and press, right side down, on a padded surface to remove the hoop marks.

COMPLETING THE TOWEL

1 Measure 3½" (8.9cm) from the 16" (40.6cm) edge near the embroidery. Pull and remove two adjacent threads, but do not cut along the resulting gap. This opening will hold the hemstitches.

2 Press ½" (1.3cm) to the wrong side on the short end near the threads pulled for hemstitching. Fold the pressed edge to meet the hemstitching gap and press again. Pin or baste the hem in place.

3 Fill needle and bobbin with lightweight heirloom thread to match the linen. Insert the wing needle and attach a zigzag or open-toe presser foot. **CAUTION:** *Do not use the machine's automatic needle threader with the wing needle.*

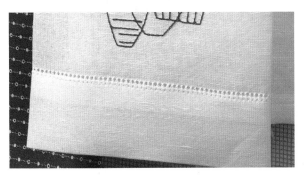

4 Choose a *point de Paris* or other heirloom hemstitch from the machine's stitch menu and sew from one side of the linen to

the other with the right side up. Position the stitch so the continuous part of the stitch falls into the gap created by the pulled threads, with the swing stitch moving to catch the folded edge of the hem. (See the photo at left for a close-up of the towel that shows this positioning.)

5 Replace the wing needle with a regular needle and thread the machine with all-purpose sewing thread to match the linen.

6 Press ½" (1.3cm) to the wrong side of the other short end, then press under another ½" (1.3cm). Repeat to press the hems on each long side of the towel.

7 Stitch the hems along the sides and the short end.

more ideas:

❖

Linen towel blanks are easy to find online. Keep a few to embellish with redwork for quick hostess gifts.

❖

Add more color by sewing a print fabric strip to the lower end of a dishtowel, just below the embroidered motif. It's a great way to use scraps from the quilts or other projects in this book!

Delightful Dishtowels

Dishtowel blanks are also easy to embellish with redwork, especially towels with a flat weave or with an inset panel for embroidery. *Towels from Charles Craft.*

Fresh Towels Every Day

Make day-of-the-week towels with the kitten designs on the CD-ROM (designs #DOW001–DOW007). *Towels from Wimpole Street.*

SILK HEARTS PILLOW

Redwork can be used to accent any pillow, but with this project you'll combine four identical motifs to create a large design that fills the pillow top with embroidery. The effect is a combination of quilt motif and kaleidoscope, and fills the entire pillow top. Fabric and thread with the lovely luster of silk combine with soft Turkish corners for an inviting boudoir accessory.

what you'll need

½ yd. (45.7cm) red silk dupioni

1 yd. (0.9m) iron-on interfacing

Embroidery*, bobbin and sewing threads

14" (35.6cm) pillow form *(Note: The pillow form is larger than the 12" [30.5cm] pillow cover to fill the depth formed by the Turkish corners.)*

Polyester fiberfill

Chalk or other removable marking tool

Template Tearaway or other template material**

YLI 50-wt. silk was used in our sample.

**Floriani Template Tearaway was used for this project (provided by RNK Distributing).*

DESIGN *on* CD-ROM

#MSC037

(see Key to Designs on CD-ROM, *pages 102–119)*

instructions

Seam allowance is ½" (1.3cm).

NOTE: *The pillow can be embroidered without using full-size templates, but using the templates makes matching the repeated design easier and more accurate.*

CUTTING THE FABRIC

1 Cut two 15" × 15" (38.1cm × 38.1cm) squares each from the dupioni and interfacing.

2 Following the manufacturer's instructions, fuse the interfacing to the wrong side of each dupioni square. **NOTE:** *No additional stabilizer is needed for embroidering redwork on the interfaced dupioni.*

EMBROIDERING THE PILLOW TOP

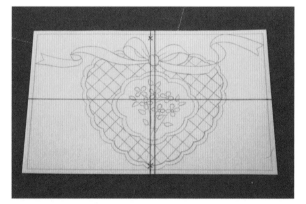

1 Print a full-size template of the embroidery design on Template Tearaway or other template material. Draw the horizontal and vertical axes on the template if the software doesn't automatically print them.

Because Design #MSC037 is not a symmetrical design, the heart's center is not the design center. Draw a new vertical axis ⅛" (3mm) to the right of the original centerline and mark the original centerline with *X*s. Both centers will be used in placing the motif on the silk.

2 Using a removable marking tool such as chalk, draw diagonal lines from corner to corner in both directions across the pillow front. Mark crosshatches on each line 2⅞" (7.3cm) from the center point (where the lines cross). These mark the centers for the four embroidery designs. **NOTE:** *Test marking choices on a fabric scrap to ensure their removability. Avoid water-soluble products, because water may leave permanent spots on the silk.*

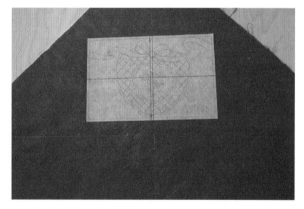

3 Peel the protective paper from the Template Tearaway and adhere the template to the pillow front, matching the *modified* design center point to the crosshatch on one diagonal.

4 Hoop the fabric with the design centered. The fabric can be hooped on the diagonal, so that the design is straight in relation to the hoop (as shown); or, if a larger hoop is available, the fabric can be hooped on the straight grain and the design rotated to match the template.

5 Use the machine's controls to position the needle exactly over the *original* design center point.

6 Remove the template. (Note that the needle drop is not aligned with the crosshatch). Embroider the design, but do **not** stitch through the Template Tearaway.

7 Repeat Steps 3–6 to embroider the design at each of the other crosshatches, rehooping as necessary and reusing the template to ensure correct positioning.

8 When the embroidery is complete, remove the markings, lay the fabric face down on a padded surface and press gently.

CONSTRUCTING THE PILLOW

1 Fold a Turkish corner (see *Making Turkish Corners,* page 84) at each corner of the pillow front. Baste the corner tucks ⅜" (9mm) from the fabric raw edges. Do not trim the excess fabric at the corners; it helps shape the finished pillow.

2 Fold Turkish corners at all four corners of the pillow back.

3 Lay the pillow back and front right sides together, matching the raw edges and corner tucks, and stitch, leaving most of one side open for stuffing. The seam line curves gently around the Turkish corners, and there is no pivoting.

4 Turn the pillow right side out and insert a pillow form, adding fiberfill as needed to fill the Turkish corners. Tuck in the seam allowances at the opening and close the pillow invisibly by hand.

DEMONSTRATION
making Turkish corners

Repeat the following instructions for each corner on the pillow front and pillow back.

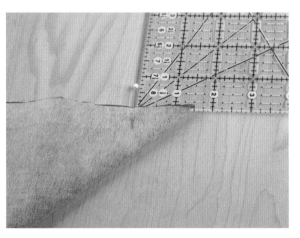

1 Fold the corner diagonally, right sides together, matching the raw edges. Place a pin 1½" (3.8cm) from the corner through both thicknesses.

2 Flatten the corner evenly across the pin, forming tucks on either side of the pin.

Wrong Side of Pinned Turkish Corner

Right Side of Pinned Turkish Corner

3 Pin each side of the kite shape formed by the tucks as shown.

more ideas:

There are many ways to combine designs for a large arrangement like this pillow. Here are some other examples.

Rotated Floral Motifs #1
Repeats of #FLW095 are rotated so leaves are on the diagonal, facing outward.

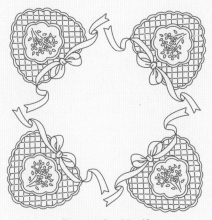

Rotate the Motif
Design #MSC037 is repeated and rotated for this grouping around a central point.

Rotated Floral Motifs #2
Here repeats of #FLW095 are rotated so the diagonally placed leaves meet at the center of the grouping.

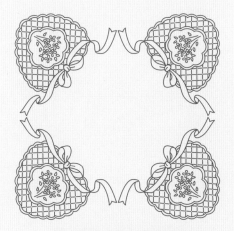

Use Both Mirror Imaging and Rotation
This creates a grouping in which repeats of #MSC037 are reversed rather than identical. The arrangement is rectangular, and adjacent ribbon ends match.

Mirrored Floral Motifs
Mirrored images of #FLW095 create this grouping. Notice the symmetrical negative space at the center.

CHRISTMAS ORNAMENTS

What could be simpler than stitching redwork on forgiving, non-raveling felt? Use this easy technique to turn any embroidered motif into a tiny hanging work of art. Accent the simple stitches with metallic threads and fancy braids; choose felted wool to add extra textural appeal. The ornaments are so quick to stitch that you'll have time to make many of them.

what you'll need

Felt or felted wool for embroidery and backing

Tear-away stabilizer

Ribbon or cord for hanging loop

Embroidery, bobbin and sewing threads

OPTIONAL

Metallic thread

Decorative braids

Embroidery digitizing software

Felted wool and Sewing Thread for our ornaments were provided by Weeks Dye Works.

Metallic braids and cords for our ornaments were provided by Kreinik Manufacturing Co., Inc.

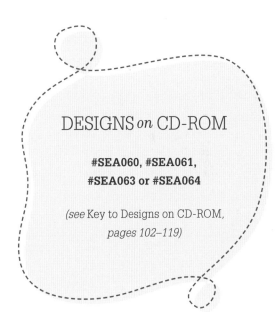

DESIGNS *on* CD-ROM

**#SEA060, #SEA061,
#SEA063 or #SEA064**

(see Key to Designs on CD-ROM,
pages 102–119)

instructions

CREATE A FRAMING SHAPE

1 In embroidery digitizing software, create a simple framing shape around the redwork motif. Use an oval, rectangle or other shape the software can apply automatically, or manually create an outline ¼" (6mm) away from the redwork edges.

2 Save the file under a new name and take it to the embroidery machine.

Outlining Tips

❀ If your digitizing software can generate decorative stitch patterns, experiment with using repeating trees, stars or other holiday motifs to stitch the outline.

❀ Some machines can add framing shapes with the machine's controls or even create a shaped outline to echo the embroidery motif. Use these options as an alternative to digitizing software, if desired.

EMBROIDERING AND CONSTRUCTING THE ORNAMENT

1 Hoop felt and stabilizer and stitch the redwork motif.

2 Slide the backing felt, right side down, under the hooped felt and stabilizer. Stitch the framing design, using bobbin thread that matches the backing felt.

Added Flair for Ornaments
Pink the edges (see snowman ornament in photo on page 86) or couch decorative braid along the ornament outline (above). *Design: #SEA060. Threads and braid: Weeks Dye Works, Kreinik Manufacturing Co., Inc.*

more ideas:

❀

*Add a puff of fiberfill before completing the stitches that attach
the backing to create an ornament with more dimension.*

❀

Consider nonseasonal designs for year-round ornaments.

❀

*Long, narrow motifs such as the Christmas bells (#SEA061)
do double duty as bookmarks (right).*

❀

*Fuse or glue the embroidered layer to handmade paper
or cardstock, write the recipient's name on the back
and the ornament becomes a clever gift tag.*

3 Remove the fabrics from the hoop. Grasp the embroidered motif and gently pull the tear-away stabilizer from the middle of the felt layers. It should tear cleanly along the stitched frame, and the stabilizer that remains inside the ornament provides extra body.

4 Trim the felt layers just outside the embroidered frame, or leave ⅛" (3mm) to ¼" (6mm) of the backing exposed beyond the top layer to create a frame around the embroidered felt. Use pinking shears, if desired, to give the ornament a decorative edge.

5 Use a large-eyed needle to thread decorative cord through the top of the ornament. Knot the cord ends to create the hanging loop.

Drawing a Stitching Line

If you prefer, use a stencil or other tool to draw a stitching line around the embroidered motif, and attach the backing felt with a sewing machine or by hand. Look for stencils and cutting templates among quilting and scrapbooking supplies to use in trimming the ornament to size.

REDWORK TABLE RUNNER

Fringed edges make this runner a quick and simple project. Arrange redwork motifs at the ends and along the long edges, leaving the center blank for a vase of flowers or decorative centerpiece. Want a longer runner? Just cut a longer rectangle and add more motifs!

what you'll need

½ yd. (45.7cm) linen, 54" (1.4m) wide

Embroidery, bobbin and sewing threads

Adhesive water-soluble stabilizer

Removable marking tool

Our table runner was embroidered with Sulky 30-wt. cotton Blendables thread.

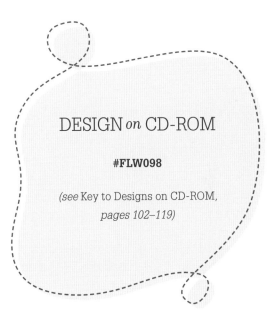

DESIGN *on* CD-ROM

#FLW098

(see Key to Designs on CD-ROM, pages 102–119)

Close-Up of Motif

This table runner uses repeats of Design #FLW098 on the ends and along the sides.
See the diagram on page 93 for embroidery placement.

instructions

CUTTING THE FABRIC

1 Cut a 16" × 45" (40.6cm × 114.3cm) rectangle from the linen.

2 Pull threads to determine the runner's edges and ensure the cuts lie on the fabric grain. See page 78 of the *Hemstitched Linen Towel* instructions for details.

EMBROIDERING THE RUNNER

1 Fold the linen rectangle in half widthwise to find the centerline and mark lines 3⅜" (8.6cm) to each side of the centerline with a removable marking tool. Draw perpendicular lines 3¼" (8.3cm) from the runner raw edges, crossing the previous lines, to indicate the centers of two embroidery repeats along each edge. (See the embroidery positioning diagram on page 93.)

2 Repeat Step 1, folding the fabric lengthwise, to mark the centers of two embroidery repeats at each end.

3 Hoop adhesive water-soluble stabilizer and remove the protective paper within the hoop. Center one design location within the hoop and attach the linen to the hooped stabilizer. Embroider the first design repeat. **NOTE:** *Use the same thread in needle and bobbin, if you prefer.*

4 Embroider the design seven more times, rehooping and replacing the stabilizer as necessary. When all embroidery is complete, trim the stabilizer close to the designs.

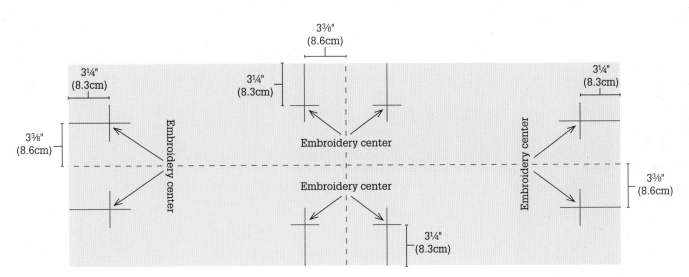

Embroidery Placement Diagram for *Redwork Table Runner*

Diagram labels:
- 3⅜" (8.6cm)
- 3¼" (8.3cm)
- 3¼" (8.3cm)
- 3¼" (8.3cm)
- 3⅜" (8.6cm)
- 3⅜" (8.6cm)
- 3¼" (8.3cm)
- Embroidery center
- Embroidery center
- Embroidery center
- Embroidery center

CONSTRUCTING THE RUNNER

1 Draw lines ½" (1.3cm) from each raw edge of the linen rectangle. Set the sewing machine for a zigzag stitch 1.5 mm wide and 1.4 mm long, and thread both needle and bobbin with all-purpose thread that matches the linen.

2 Sew along each line, pivoting at the corners. Position the zigzag stitches directly on the guidelines.

3 Fringe the runner edges by removing warp or weft threads parallel to each line of zigzag stitches.

4 Rinse and soak the runner in plain water to remove the markings and the water-soluble stabilizer. When all stabilizer is gone, roll the runner in a towel and squeeze to remove the excess moisture. Press the runner while the linen is slightly damp, using spray starch if desired.

more ideas:

❀

Look for blank table runners that are ready to embellish.

❀

Stitch matching motifs on placemats and napkins for a complete table setting.

Blanks Embroidered with Motifs from CD-ROM
Designs: #FLW090–#FLW093. Blank table linens from Wimpole Street.

FRAMED SENTIMENTS

Sometimes a frame is all that's needed to complete an embroidered motif. For an even more personal touch, add letters to spell a name, express a sentiment or create a modern version of the traditional alphabet sampler. Look for frames in interesting shapes and colors, and plan the embroidery to fit the frame.

what you'll need

Medium-weight fabric for embroidery*

Embroidery and bobbin threads

Iron-on tear-away stabilizer

Needlework mounting board, or artist's illustration board and double-sided adhesive tape
(see Mounting Board note on page 97)

Frames

OPTIONAL

Brown paper

Hanging hardware (sawtooth hanger, wire and eyelets, etc.)

* Heavier fabrics render the mounted embroidery too large to fit the frame.

DESIGNS *on* CD-ROM

used in samples:
#HOM085 (page 94);
#NOS049 (page 97);
#ANI036, #FOM008,
#FOM010, #FOM014 and
#HOM082 (page 97, montage)

(see Key to Designs on CD-ROM, pages 102–119)

instructions

CREATING THE SENTIMENTS

1 Decide which motif(s) to use. Choose an embroidery font for accompanying letters.

2 Choose a size for the finished embroidery. To keep the cost low, plan to fit the redwork and lettering into a standard frame size such as 5" × 7" (12.7cm × 17.8cm) or 8" × 10" (20.3cm × 25.4cm). For machine embroidery, also keep the embroidery hoop size in mind, and plan to split the complete design into hoop-sized sections if necessary.

3 Open the redwork motif in embroidery software or at the machine's controls. Import the lettering and arrange it as desired. Save the complete design with a new file name, splitting it as necessary to fit the embroidery hoop. Another option is to print full-size templates of the redwork and any letters that will be added, grouping the letters into words or phrases as much as possible. Arrange the templates on the background fabric and use them to mark embroidery placements for each design element.

4 Stabilize the fabric and embroider the design. Remove the excess stabilizer when the embroidery is complete, and carefully press the embroidery from the wrong side on a towel or padded surface.

Lettering Tip

Consider these possibilities as you arrange the lettering: centering, arcing or using multiple font sizes to emphasize some words. Remember that words can be placed above and below the motif, or to one side.

Choosing Fonts for Embroidery

Embroidery fonts can be purchased from a variety of sources, and most embroidery machines have one or more built-in fonts. Look for true fonts that can be typed continuously to form words, rather than monogram collections comprising individual letters.

Digitizing software can be used to create lettering, too. Some programs allow access to all the TrueType fonts on the computer, automatically converting them to stitches.

Choose a font compatible with redwork, such as running-stitch letters or an outline-only font. Use software or machine features to arrange the letters in an arc or other complementary shape, and select a font size that will not overpower the redwork motif.

For hand embroidery, use a word processing or graphics program to choose a font and arrange and size the words. Print the result and use it as the embroidery pattern.

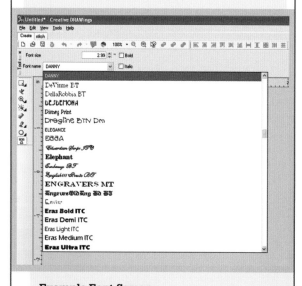

Example Font Screen
The most helpful programs provide a preview of each font in the list.

more ideas:

❀

Choose a design that coordinates with a hobby or special interest (such as Model Airplanes in the sample, near right) and personalize the embroidery for a lucky recipient.

❀

Words aren't always necessary, as seen in this montage of florals and herbals (far right). Pick an interesting frame and let it guide your choice of theme and designs to embroider.

MOUNTING THE SENTIMENT

1 Cut the mounting board or illustration board to fit the chosen frame. Lay the board on the embroidery wrong side, centering the embroidery. Trim the embroidered fabric at least 1" (2.5cm) larger on all sides than the mounting board.

2 To secure the embroidery to the mounting board, remove the protective paper to expose the adhesive surface. Beginning at the center of the board and the embroidery, smooth the fabric onto the board, keeping the grain straight and the embroidery centered. Turn the embroidery right side down and wrap the fabric raw edges tightly around the board's edges. Use glue or double-sided tape to secure the edges to the back of the board, folding the corners at an angle to minimize fabric thickness.

Follow the manufacturer's instructions to use needlework mounting tape and nonadhesive board instead.

3 Remove the backing cardboard, filler papers and glass from the picture frame.

4 Place the mounted needlework in the frame, followed by the cardboard backing. Leave the glass out of the frame to provide space for the embroidery and to protect the fabric from damage that can occur when the textile is in direct contact with a glass pane.

5 **Optional:** Cut a piece of brown paper ⅛" (3mm) smaller on each side than the outside frame dimensions from a shopping bag or roll of craft paper . Glue the paper to the frame back, covering the wrong side, to seal out dust.

6 Add a hanger or hanging wire to the frame's wrong side if needed.

Mounting Board

Needlework mounting board is available at most sewing and craft retailers. It has one adhesive surface, covered by protective paper, for holding the embroidery in place. The board is available in standard frame sizes and can be cut with a craft knife to fit nonstandard frames.

Illustration board is found with mat board at art and craft retailers. Pair nonadhesive illustration board with double-sided adhesive tape specially made for mounting needlework, available from needlework shops and online retailers, as a substitute for mounting board.

the designs on cd-rom

One hundred motifs from *The WORK-BASKET* magazine are included on the CD-ROM accompanying this book. The designs are presented in a variety of formats for both hand and machine embroiderers. A thumbnail index of the designs appears on pages 102-119.

The designs are organized into ten broad categories: *Animals*, *Days of the Week Cats*, *Flowers*, *Flowers of the Month*, *Fruits and Veggies*, *Hearth and Home*, *Juvenile*, *Miscellaneous*, *Nostalgia* and *Seasonal*. With motifs for men, women and children, there's something for everyone.

Key to Designs on CD-ROM (pages 102-119) includes dimensions for the machine embroidery designs. The graphics files for hand embroiderers on the CD-ROM, in contrast, present the motifs at their original sizes from *The WORKBASKET*'s iron-on transfers.

Feel free to substitute designs for those shown in the book's projects. Arrange and resize the motifs, or stitch them in different colors on varied fabrics. With one hundred choices, the sky's the limit!

Using the CD-ROM

All one hundred designs are presented on the CD-ROM in seven common machine embroidery formats: ART, DST, EXP, HUS, JEF, PES and VP3. If a different file format is needed, use design conversion software to convert one of these formats into the one you require. Eighty-five of the designs will fit within a 4" × 4" (100mm × 100mm) machine embroidery hoop, while the other fifteen designs require a hoop at least 5" × 7" (130mm × 180mm).

Usually a collection of machine embroidery designs also includes text files that specify the color stops, or color changes, in the motif. Because these designs are all single-color embroideries, those text files are not included. A few designs, such as the Flowers of the Month, are digitized with two color stops to facilitate stitching the motifs with or without the accompanying words, but even those designs can be stitched in just one color.

DESIGNS FOR HAND EMBROIDERY

All designs are stored on the CD-ROM in JPEG format as well. This is a graphics format that is recognized by many computer programs, including Paint, Photoshop Elements and Paint Shop Pro. Use the JPEG images to create mirror images for design transfers, print the JPEGs with your computer printer, and rescale the designs to create hand embroidery motifs in different sizes.

In addition, all designs are also presented in PDF format on the CD-ROM. Portable Document Format (PDF) files are recognized by Adobe Acrobat Reader (free software is available at www.adobe.com). The Reader is used by many companies and may be installed already on your computer. Files in PDF format are especially easy to open and print.

Previewing Designs on Quilts

One reason the designs are included on the CD-ROM in EXP format is the feature of Electric Quilt's latest versions that allows users to preview embroidery designs on their quilt layouts. Even if you don't have an embroidery machine or embroidery software, the EXP files can be imported by EQ and displayed in Layer 3 of a quilt project.

For full instructions, consult the EQ manual.

***Circus Wall Quilt* Previewed in Electric Quilt**
Image created with Electric Quilt 6.

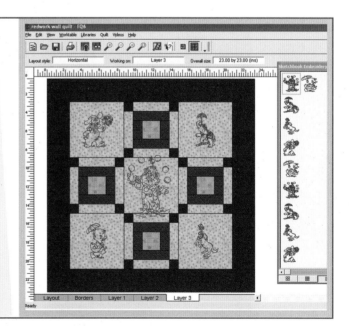

Special Notes on These Designs

When a digitizer creates a machine embroidery design from scratch, he skillfully crafts the design lines to avoid jump stitches and arranges the colors so traveling stitches can be hidden under layers of fill.

By contrast, these authentic *WORKBASKET®* designs for hand embroidery originally were created with the idea that a skillful stitcher could tie off her thread whenever necessary, or simply bring the thread to the back of the work and move to another area of the design.

To maintain the character and detail of these motifs from another era, the machine embroidery files on the enclosed CD-ROM include more jump stitches than usual.

Some jumps have been deliberately exaggerated to make them easier to clip. For example, look at the before and after photographs below of design #FRV025. After stitching a detail line, the needle jumps away from the design, then returns to stitch the next detail line. It looks messy when stitched, but the jump stitches are obvious and easier to trim.

When clipping jump stitches, trim the needle thread close to the design stitches, but leave at least ⅛" (3mm) of bobbin thread at each end of the jump on the wrong side. If the jumps aren't too long and the back of the design will be covered in the finished project, simply leave the bobbin thread intact. If a tear-away stabilizer was used, carefully remove the stabilizer before trimming the jump stitches. These strategies help ensure that the small detail lines won't pull out of the fabric as the jump stitches are cut.

For projects that will be subject to wear and tear, place a tiny drop of seam sealant on the bobbin thread at each end of the jump stitch and allow it to dry before clipping the threads. Be sure to test first on a sample of the fabric and thread, to be sure the seam sealant won't stain the fabric.

Some of the stitches in these redwork designs are very short in order to duplicate the curves and other small details of the original motifs. For the best quality stitchout, follow one or more of these suggestions:
- Loosen the tension on the needle thread.
- Slow the machine speed.
- Use matching thread in the bobbin, either the same thread used in the needle or bobbin thread in a matching color.

Finally, remember it's always a good idea to stitch a sample on scrap fabric first to test the interaction of the design, machine and thread.

Before and After
The stitched motif at left shows the jump stitches untrimmed; the motif at right shows the finished design with threads clipped. *Design: #FRV025.*

Key to Designs on CD-ROM

On the following pages, you'll find thumbnails of one hundred designs from *The WORKBASKET®*. These are the same designs available on the enclosed CD-ROM as computer graphics files and machine embroidery designs. For more information about the CD-ROM contents, see pages 100-101.

Accompanying each design is a brief notation including the design file name and the machine embroidery design size.

NOTE: *There may be slight variations in the dimensions among formats.*

animals

#ANI029
5.50" × 4.57" (14cm × 11.6cm)

#ANI028
4.24" × 6.71" (10.8cm × 17cm)

#ANI030
2.70" × 2.66" (6.9cm × 6.8cm)

#ANI031
3.17" × 3.71" (8cm × 9.4cm)

#ANI034
2.20" × 0.96" (5.6cm × 2.4cm)

#ANI032
1.97" × 1.62" (5cm × 4.1cm)

#ANI035
3.75" × 0.74" (9.5cm × 1.9cm)

#ANI033
2.48" × 2.53" (6.3cm × 6.4cm)

#ANI036
3.71" × 1.66" (9.4cm × 4.2cm)

days of the week cats

THURSDAY

#DOW005

1.83" × 3.75" (4.6cm × 9.5cm)

SUNDAY

#DOW001

2.69" × 3.75" (6.8cm × 9.5cm)

TUESDAY

#DOW003

2.65" × 3.75" (6.7cm × 9.5cm)

MONDAY

#DOW002

3.05" × 3.74" (7.7cm × 9.5cm)

WEDNESDAY

#DOW004

3.02" × 3.74" (7.7cm × 9.5cm)

FRIDAY

#DOW006

2.07" × 3.75" (5.3cm × 9.5cm)

SATURDAY

#DOW007

2.56" × 3.77" (6.5cm × 9.6cm)

flowers

#FLW090
3.13" × 3.70" (7.9cm × 9.4cm)

#FLW092
3.70" × 3.39" (9.4cm × 8.6cm)

#FLW091
3.57" × 3.72" (9.1cm × 9.4cm)

#FLW093
3.49" × 3.70" (8.9cm × 9.4cm)

#FLW094
6.69" × 2.58" (17cm × 6.5cm)

#FLW095
3.27" × 2.31" (8.3cm × 5.9cm)

#FLW096
6.67" × 3.31" (16.9cm × 8.4cm)

#FLW098
6.69" × 4.13" (17cm × 10.5cm)

#FLW097
3.72" × 3.06" (9.4cm × 7.8cm)

#FLW099
2.22" × 2.50" (5.6cm × 6.3cm)

#FLW100
3.70" × 3.46" (9.4cm × 8.8cm)

flowers of the month

JANUARY   CARNATION
#FOM008
2.70" × 3.68" (6.9cm × 9.3cm)

FEBRUARY

VIOLET
#FOM009
2.79" × 3.83" (7.1cm × 9.7cm)

MARCH
SWEET PEA
#FOM010
2.72" × 3.82" (6.9cm × 9.7cm)

APRIL
JONQUIL
#FOM011
3.13" × 3.81" (7.9cm × 9.7cm)

MAY
LILY-OF-THE-VALLEY
#FOM012
3.14" × 3.83" (7.8cm × 9.7cm)

JUNE
ROSE
#FOM013
2.31" × 3.82" (5.9cm × 9.7cm)

JULY   LARKSPUR
#FOM014
2.58" × 3.70" (6.5cm × 9.4cm)

AUGUST
GLADIOLUS
#FOM015
2.53" × 3.90" (6.4cm × 9.9cm)

SEPTEMBER
ASTER
#FOM016
2.74" × 3.81" (6.9cm × 9.7cm)

OCTOBER
CALENDULA
#FOM017
2.85" × 3.82" (7.2cm × 9.7cm)

NOVEMBER
#FOM018
2.81" × 3.80" (7.1cm × 9.6cm)

DECEMBER
NARCISSIS
#FOM019
2.42" × 3.79" (6.1cm × 9.6cm)

fruits and veggies

#FRV020
3.02" × 3.74" (7.7cm × 9.5cm)

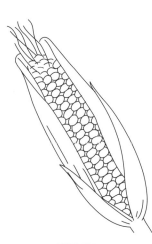

#FRV021
2.72" × 3.82" (6.9cm × 9.7cm)

#FRV022
3.72" × 3.80" (9.4cm × 9.6cm)

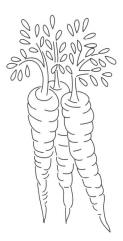

#FRV023
2.01" × 3.82" (5.1cm × 9.7cm)

#FRV024
2.31" × 3.75" (5.9cm × 9.5cm)

#FRV025
2.92" × 3.82" (7.4cm × 9.7cm)

#FRV026
3.16" × 3.35" (8.1cm × 8.4cm)

#FRV027
3.81" × 3.57" (9.7cm × 9.1cm)

hearth and home

#HOM078
2.54" × 3.72" (6.3cm × 9.4cm)

#HOM079
2.81" × 3.70" (7.1cm × 9.4cm)

#HOM080
2.52" × 3.73" (6.3cm × 9.4cm)

#HOM081
2.10" × 3.74" (5.3cm × 9.5cm)

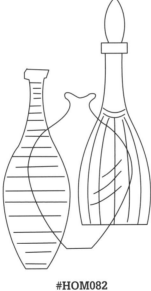

#HOM082
2.09" × 3.78" (5.3cm × 9.6cm)

#HOM083
1.31" × 3.77" (3.3cm × 9.6cm)

#HOM084
3.78" × 3.03" (9.6cm × 7.6cm)

#HOM085
3.28" × 2.76" (8.4cm × 7.1cm)

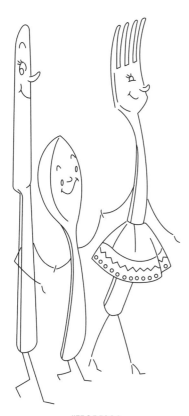

#HOM086
1.75" × 3.89" (4.3cm × 9.9cm)

#HOM087
3.74" × 2.25" (9.5cm × 5.6cm)

#HOM088
3.54" × 2.49" (8.9cm × 6.3cm)

#HOM089
3.71" × 3.36" (9.4cm × 8.6cm)

juvenile

#JUV066

2.68" × 3.82" (6.9cm × 9.7cm)

#JUV067

1.72" × 3.82" (4.3cm × 9.7cm)

#JUV068

3.74" × 3.21" (9.5cm × 8.1cm)

#JUV069

3.84" × 3.50" (9.6cm × 8.9cm)

#JUV070

3.74" × 3.61" (9.5cm × 9.1cm)

#JUV071

2.44" × 3.74" (6.1cm × 9.5cm)

#JUV072
4.83" × 6.83" (12.2cm × 17.3cm)

#JUV075
3.13" × 3.86" (7.9cm × 9.6cm)

#JUV076
2.26" × 3.74" (5.8cm × 9.5cm)

#JUV073
2.29" × 3.82" (5.8cm × 9.7cm)

#JUV074
2.55" × 3.83" (6.3cm × 9.7cm)

#JUV077
3.35" × 3.87" (8.4cm × 9.6cm)

miscellaneous

#MSC037
6.69" × 4.32" (17cm × 10.9cm)

#MSC038
6.71" × 1.90" (17cm × 4.8cm)

#MSC039
6.39" × 4.75" (16.3cm × 11.9cm)

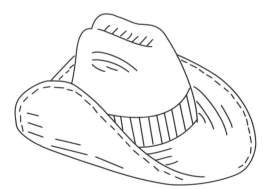

#MSC040
3.30" × 2.24" (8.4cm × 5.6cm)

#MSC041
4.83" × 4.06" (12.2cm × 10.4cm)

#MSC044
4.68" × 4.80" (11.9cm × 12.2cm)

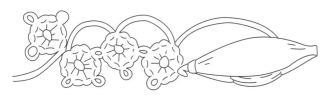

#MSC042
3.67" × 3.74" (9.4cm × 9.5cm)

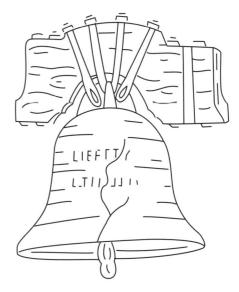

#MSC045
3.15" × 3.82" (7.9cm × 9.7cm)

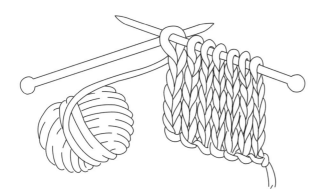

#MSC043
3.82" × 2.23" (9.7cm × 5.6cm)

#MSC046
2.91" × 3.82" (7.4cm × 9.7cm)

#MSC047
3.77" × 6.57" (9.6cm × 16.8cm)

#MSC048
2.20" × 3.82" (5.6cm × 9.7cm)

#NOS049
3.76" × 1.98" (9.6cm × 5.1cm)

nostalgia

#NOS050
3.82" × 3.63" (9.7cm × 9.1cm)

#NOS052
2.46" × 3.82" (6.3cm × 9.7cm)

#NOS051
3.82" × 2.67" (9.7cm × 6.9cm)

#NOS053
2.47" × 3.82" (6.3cm × 9.7cm)

#NOS054
2.95" × 3.82" (7.4cm × 9.7cm)

#NOS057
5.50" × 4.33" (14cm × 10.9cm)

#NOS055
2.72" × 3.82" (6.9cm × 9.7cm)

#NOS058
3.09" × 3.82" (7.9cm × 9.7cm)

#NOS056
2.28" × 2.15" (5.8cm × 5.3cm)

seasonal

#SEA059
5.65" × 4.75" (14.2cm × 11.9cm)

#SEA060
2.34" × 3.74" (5.8cm × 9.5cm)

#SEA061
1.52" × 3.75" (3.8cm × 9.5cm)

#SEA062

6.69" × 1.96" (17cm × 5.1cm)

#SEA063

1.88" × 2.55" (4.8cm × 6.3cm)

#SEA065

3.75" × 3.46" (9.5cm × 8.8cm)

#SEA064

2.09" × 2.46" (5.3cm × 6.3cm)

subject index to designs on cd-rom

A

airplane, #NOS049

Animals, #ANI028–ANI036. *See also* #DOW001–DOW007, #JUV069, #JUV071, #JUV073–JUV077

animated kitchenware, #HOM086–#HOM089

antique car, #NOS050, #NOS051

antique telephone, #NOS055

apple, #FRV025

April, #FOM011

Asian, #MSC046, #MSC047

aster, #FOM016

August, #FOM015

B

baby carriage, #NOS056

bells, #SEA061

bicycle built for two, #NOS054

birds, #ANI030, #ANI031, #ANI033, #ANI036, #FLW097, #HOM084, #HOM085, #MSC044

boot with flowers, #FLW099

bottles/vases, #HOM082

bunny, #JUV071

butter churn with ivy, #HOM081

butterfly, #ANI032

butterfly border, #ANI035

C

calendula, #FOM017

campfire cookout, #MSC039

car, old-fashioned, #NOS050, #NOS051

carnation, #FOM008

carrots, #FRV023

cats, #DOW001–DOW007, #JUV077

cherries, #FRV026

chicken covered dish, #HOM084, #HOM085

chickens, #ANI030, #ANI031, #HOM084, #HOM085

china, animated, #HOM087–#HOM089

Chinese guardian lion, #MSC046

Christmas, #SEA061–#SEA064

chrysanthemum, #FOM018

chives, #FLW091

circus, #JUV072–#JUV074

clown, #JUV072

coffee pot, #MSC039, #HOM080

cookout, campfire, #MSC039

corn, #FRV021

cornucopia, #SEA059

couple, old-fashioned, #NOS054, #NOS058

couple, #NOS054, #NOS057, #NOS058

covered dish, chicken, #HOM084, #HOM085

covered dish, hen, #HOM085

covered dish, rooster #HOM084

cowboy hat, #MSC040

cowboy, #JUV066

creamer, animated, #HOM088

D

daffodils and hyacinths, #FLW100

dancing couple, #NOS057

Days of the Week Cats, #DOW001–DOW007

days of the week, #DOW001–DOW007

December, #FOM019

dishes, animated, #HOM087–#HOM089

dog, #ANI029

dogwood blossom, #FLW095

dogwood blossoms grouping, #FLW096

duckling, #JUV076

E

eagle, Federal, #MSC044

elephant, #JUV073

embroidered heart, #MSC037

F

February, #FOM009

Federal eagle, #MSC044

fisherman, #MSC048

flatware, animated, #HOM086

flowers in boot, #FLW099

flowers in swan, #FLW097

Flowers of the Month, #FOM008–FOM019

Flowers, #FLW090–FLW100. *See also* #FOM008-FOM019

folk art couple, #NOS057

Foo dog, #MSC046

fork, animated, #HOM086

Friday, #DOW006

Fruits and Veggies, #FRV020–FRV027

fruits, #FRV020, #FRV025–#FRV027, #SEA059

G

garland, holly, #SEA062

gladiolus, #FOM015

grapes, #FRV020

H

heart, #MSC037, #SEA065

Hearth and Home, #HOM078–HOM089

hen covered dish, #HOM085

hen, #ANI030, #HOM085

herbs, #FLW090–FLW093

holiday bells, #SEA061

holly garland, #SEA062

home and hearth, #HOM078–HOM089

horse, #JUV074

horse head, #ANI028

Quilt Layout Diagrams

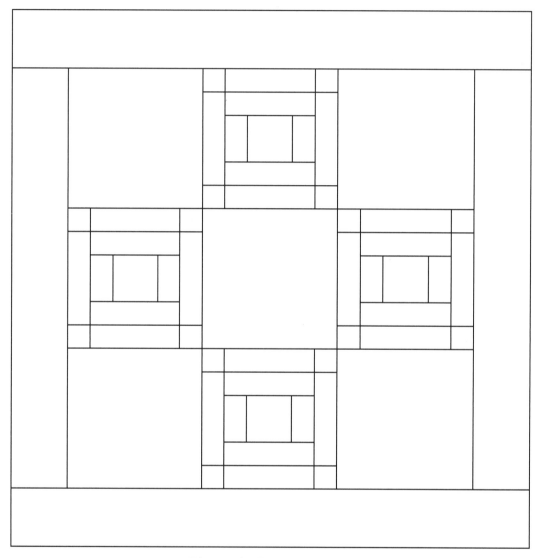

Diagram for *Circus Wall Quilt*
Page 52

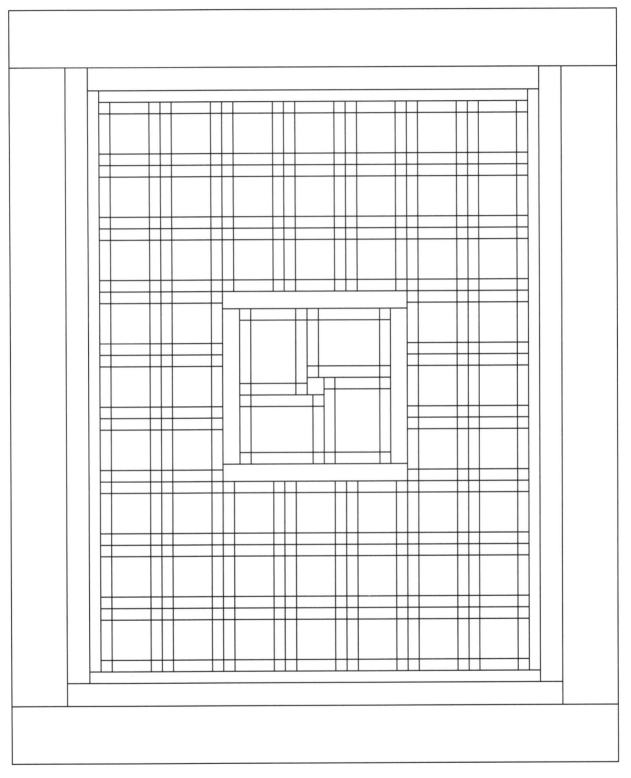

Diagram for *Redwork Quilt*

Page 36

RESOURCES

BLANKS

All About Blanks
www.allaboutblanks.com

Charles Craft
www.charlescraft.com

Wimpole Street
www.wimpolestreet.com
www.barrett-house.com (distributor)

FABRICS

**Paintbrush Studio Collections,
a division of Fabri-Quilt, Inc.**
www.fabri-quilt.com

**NOTIONS, THREADS
AND SOFTWARE**

Brother International
www.brothersews.com

Coats & Clark
www.coatsandclark.com

Creative DRAWings
www.creative-drawings.com

DMC
www.dmc-usa.com

The Electric Quilt Company
www.electricquilt.com

Floriani Products/RNK Distributing
www.rnkdistributing.com

Kreinik Manufacturing Co., Inc.
www.kreinik.com

Pentel Arts
www.pentelarts.com

Sulky of America
www.sulky.com

The Warm Company
www.warmcompany.com

Weeks Dye Works, Inc.
www.weeksdyeworks.com

YLI
www.ylicorp.com

Long Arm Quilting
Aunt Lynn's Long Arm Quilting
423-337-9627
AuntLynnsQuilts@cs.com

FURTHER READING

The Embroidery Stitch Bible
by Betty Barnden

*Fill in the Blanks
with Machine Embroidery*
by Rebecca Kemp Brent

*Machine Embroidery
Wild & Wacky*
by Linda Turner Griepentrog and
Rebecca Kemp Brent

*Machine Embroidery with
Confidence, A Beginner's Guide*
by Nancy Zieman

All books by Krause Publications,
available at your local craft retailer,
bookstore or online supplier, or visit
www.mycraftivitystore.com.

about Rebecca Kemp Brent

Rebecca Kemp Brent is a freelance writer, educator and designer specializing in creative ways to use computerized sewing and embroidery machines and software.

Her titles for Krause Publications (an imprint of F+W Media, Inc.) include *Fill in the Blanks with Machine Embroidery* (2007) and *Machine Embroidery Wild & Wacky* (2006), which she coauthored with Linda Turner Griepentrog. She lives in East Tennessee and works from her home.

Rebecca began her career as a sewing educator more than 35 years ago and has also worked in theatrical costuming and apparel manufacturing.

Since 2001, she has published over a hundred and fifty articles in such national publications as *Creative Machine Embroidery*, *Sew News*, *Sewing Savvy* and *Quilting & Embroidery*, as well as on the Internet and TV. She is the designer of the 2-4-6-8 Pocket Bag Collection pattern and has created embroidery motifs for several Sudberry House collections for both hand and machine embroidery. Visit her Web site at http://rkbrent.com.

Index

READY FOR MORE MACHINE EMBROIDERY?
CHECK OUT THESE TITLES!

Machine Embroidery Wild & Wacky
STITCH ON ANY AND EVERY SURFACE

Linda Turner Griepentrog and Rebecca Kemp Brent

Machine embroidery meets true innovation in this one-of-a-kind book. With a focus on originality and experimentation, this guide covers use of unconventional bases such as wood and canvas, multiple techniques including embossing and painting and other media such as feathers and photo transfers. Add a little attitude to your next machine embroidery project with this wild guide!

paperback; 128 pages; #MEWA / ISBN-10: 0-89689-277-8 / ISBN-13: 978-0-89689-277-4

Fill in the Blanks with Machine Embroidery

Rebecca Kemp Brent

The author provides expert tips, tricks and ideas for finding blanks in shops and online, then using them to get the most out of your embroidery machine. The accompanying CD-ROM includes 13 step-by-step projects, from home decor and seasonal items to baby gifts, plus 53 beautiful embroidery designs in all machine formats.

paperback; 48 pages; #Z0747 / ISBN-10: 0-89689-483-5 / ISBN-13: 978-0-89689-483-9

Asian-Inspired Machine Embroidery

Joan Elliott

A known designer in embroidery and cross-stitch, author Joan Elliott brings 35+ classic Asian motifs to machine embroidery. All designs are included on the CD-ROM that accompanies the book, each digitized for machine embroidery in multiple formats. Black- and-white PDFs are provided as well so hand-embroiderers can create their own transfers. The book's 24 projects demonstrate how to use designs in greeting cards, a banner, table linens, garden accessories and more.

paperback; 128 pages; #Z3752 / ISBN-10: 0-89689-954-3 / ISBN-13: 978-0-89689-954-4